Excellence in the Science of Tajwīd

Daybreak Press
3533 Lexington Avenue North, Arden Hills, MN 55126
www.rabata.org/daybreakpress | daybreakpress@rabata.org

ISBN (print): 978-1-967369-02-7

Cover design: Zainab Arshad
Typesetting: Islam Farid | Islamfarid.net

Printed in the United States of America

rabata
Daybreak Press

Excellence in the Science of Tajwīd

GHADA SALAHI AL-ASBAHI

BA in Islamic Studies
Certified in the Ten Quranic Recitations

بسم الله الرحمن الرحيم

قال الله ﷻ:

﴿ٱلَّذِينَ ءَاتَيۡنَٰهُمُ ٱلۡكِتَٰبَ يَتۡلُونَهُۥ حَقَّ تِلَاوَتِهِۦٓ أُوْلَٰٓئِكَ يُؤۡمِنُونَ بِهِۦۗ
وَمَن يَكۡفُرۡ بِهِۦ فَأُوْلَٰٓئِكَ هُمُ ٱلۡخَٰسِرُونَ ١٢١﴾

Allah ﷻ has said:

Those to whom We have given the book recite it as it should be recited, they are the ones that believe therein. Those who reject faith therein are the losers.

(Al-Baqarah 121)

Contents

1 Foreword
3 Preface
5 Commonly Asked Questions
9 Biographies of Notable *Tajwīd* Scholars
12 The Science of *Tajwīd*
15 The Etiquette of Quran Recitation
18 Modes of Recitation
19 Beginning Recitation
22 The *Makhārij*
27 The *Makhārij* Based on Location
31 How to Pronounce...
32 *Ṣifāt* (The Characteristics of Articulation)
40 The Duration of the Letters
41 The Rules of *Mīm* and *Nūn*
48 The Rules of *Rā'* as They Pertain to *Tafkhīm* and *Tarqīq*

51 The Rules of *Lām* in the Name of Allah Pertaining to *Tafkhīm* and *Tarqīq*

52 The Rules of the Definitive Article *Lām* as it Relates to *Idghām* and *Iẓhār*

54 The Rules of the *Lām* When It Occurs in a Verb

55 *Idghām* as Related to *Ṣifāt*

60 The Rules of *Madd* (Elongation)

69 The Seven *Alifs*

70 Subtle Pauses (*al-Sakta al-Laṭīfa*)

72 The Two *Hamzas*: *Waṣl* and *Qaṭʿa*

75 *Waqf* (Stopping) and *Ibtidāʾ* (Starting)

80 *Ishmām* and *Rawm*

83 Symbols for Stops and Other Technical Indicators

85 The Design of the *Muṣḥaf*

86 Gross and Subtle Error

87 Notes Pertaining to the Recitation of *Ḥafṣ*

89 General Notes

92 That Which Helps in the Memorization of Quran

94 The *Dua* of Completing the Quran

95 The *Dua* for Not Forgetting What Has Been Memorized of the Quran

بسم الله الرحمن الرحيم

وبعد مقدار زارتني في البيت الآنسة غادة بنت الحاج عبد الرزاق الصلاحي الأصبحي مصطحبة رسالة كتبتها في علم التجويد.

والآنسة جامعة للقراءة العشر على المقرئ الكبير ابو حسن محي الدين الكردي وحمد لله تعالى.

وقد تصفحت هذه الرسالة فرأيت انها اجتهدت في كتابتها و حاولت فيها العبارة السهلة كما حاولت الإحاطة بكل ما يحتاجه الطالب او الطالبة في علم التجويد و قد حاولت ان تأتي برسوم مبسطة تعين الطالب على النطق مضافا ذلك إلى التلقي.

و لم تشبع كتابها بكثرة الرسوم و لا بزيادة الأمثلة ولا كثرة التبرير حرصا على عدم الملل.

و كانت ذات ذوق في كتابتها فلم تكن مطيلة بحيث تُمِلّ ولا مقتضبة بحيث تُخلّ بل كانت تخاطب القراء حين تقرأ رسالتها و كأنها تشاوره.

جزاها الله خيرا و نفع بها و الله ولي التوفيق

Foreword

بسم الله الرحمن الرحيم *In the name of Allah, the Merciful, the Compassionate.*

Anse Ghada, the daughter of Hajj Abdul Razzq Salahi Al-Asbahi, visited me in my home, bringing with her a manuscript that she wrote on the science of *tajwīd.*

Our female teacher has been authorized to transmit in the ten narrations of the Quran by the Grand Muqri᾽ Abu al-Hasan Muhyi ad-Deen al-Kurdi (may the Mercy of Allah be upon him).

I have reviewed this manuscript and have observed that much diligent effort has been put forth in its composition. Anse Ghada has provided a comprehensive overview using simple terminology in order for the student to learn the science of *tajwīd.* She has also attempted to include simplified diagrams in order to assist the student in acquiring pronunciation and comprehension skills.

Her writing takes into account the readers' needs and interest. She has avoided the overuse of diagrams, for example, and dividing the manuscript into too many chapters. Her style of writing is polished. It is neither too lengthy such that the reader may lose interest, nor is it too brief.

May God reward her greatly and benefit others with her effort for God is the Guardian of Prosperity.

Krayim Rajih

Grand Quranic Reciter of Damascus
Damascus | Rajab 13, 1433 | June 16, 2012

Preface

بسم الله الرحمن الرحيم *In the name of Allah, the Merciful, the Compassionate.*

Praise to God who began His book with praise and who rewards those who read it. Praise to God who has endowed the nation of Muhammad with the Magnificent Quran and has granted this nation that which He has not given anyone else. He has created the Quran as a guide for all of His creation; it is eternal and protected until the Day of Judgment, as He has declared.

إِنَّا نَحۡنُ نَزَّلۡنَا ٱلذِّكۡرَ وَإِنَّا لَهُۥ لَحَٰفِظُونَ ٩

We have, indeed, sent down the remembrance, and We shall preserve it. (al-Ḥijr 9)

Peace and blessings upon the one whose conduct and manners were reminiscent of the Quran, and whose testament and legacy were the Quran, the one who said, "God, the most Exalted, has a family among the people." They asked, "Who are they, O Messenger of God?" He ﷺ said, "The people of Quran are the people of God, and His elite."[1]

We have presented an abridged book in the science of *tajwīd* to the younger generation, those eager to learn *tajwīd.* I have ensured that the information is presented in a simplified yet precise and clear method. The book provides an explanation for the proper pronunciation and attributes of the letters and the rules of *tajwīd*, specifically in the narration of Ḥafṣ ʿan ʿĀṣim of the Shāṭibiyya method. I have included lines from the introduction of "al-Jazarīyya" by Imam Shams al-Dīn Muḥammad ibn Muḥammad al-Jazarī al-Dimashqī for the purpose of enforcing

---

[1] *Sunan Ibn Māja,* vol. 1, chap. 16, "The Virtues of Learning the Quran." The hadith is considered *ṣaḥīḥ* in *Majmaʿ al-zawāʾid.*

and simplifying the rules for the reader, making it easier for memorization. I have also briefly explained some of the lines using the "Explanation of the Jazarīyya" by the Islamic scholar, Zakariyya al-Anṣārī. The *tajwīd* concepts and rules are further clarified through practical examples, explanations, and illustrative charts.

The book begins with a brief biography of the following eminent scholars: ʿĀṣim, Ḥafṣ, al-Shāṭibī, and Ibn al-Jazarī.

The book has been assessed and edited by our respected scholar, Shaykh Krayim Rajih, the grand Quranic reciter of Damascus, may God reward and protect him, and keep him as a source of benefit for the Muslims.

I ask God, the most Exalted, to accept my work and benefit students who seek knowledge. I ask Him to guide us to the service of the Quran and make our deeds sincere, seeking only His path; He is Near and answers our call. Praise to the Lord of the universe.

Ghada Salahi al-Asbahi

June 1, 2012

Commonly Asked Questions

What is *tajwīd*?

Tajwīd is the science of reading the Quran correctly. Learning it is, as mentioned in this book, an obligatory act upon every Muslim. In other words, whoever reads the Quran is required to read it correctly. The science of *tajwīd* teaches all believers how to fulfill this obligation.

How should I use this book?

This is a book for students who are serious about fulfilling their obligation to the Quran and willing to seek out help from a qualified teacher. It is a translation of a detailed presentation of *tajwīd*. It is meant as an explanation to the student, not a guide. *Tajwīd* is, was, and always will be a science that cannot be learned from a book. One must listen to a correct recitation and be critically listened to, in order to follow the path of correct recitation of the Quran.

This, unfortunately, is difficult for modern Muslims, who generally enjoy being independent, are proud of their vast library of Islamic books, and feel quite confident in their ability to grow spiritually without guidance. A serious student of *tajwīd* must be just that—a student.

How do I find a qualified teacher?

This is a serious question, because wrapped up in the perils of trying to go it alone is the worse danger of being taught incorrectly. It is extremely difficult to unlearn; it is much easier to learn correctly the first time. Converts and non-native speakers be forewarned—do not assume that anyone who speaks Arabic or claims to have studied *tajwīd* in school is an appropriate teacher. Seek out a properly qualified teacher and avoid the serious consequences of learning it wrong the first time around. Today it is not difficult to find people who have an *ijāza* or are certified *tajwīd* teachers. If one does not live in your area, either study with someone who definitely understands and has studied *tajwīd*, or make plans to take a *tajwīd* vacation (travel in search of a teacher). The teacher will be the director and guide, but, in the end, it is still the student who has to do the work.

Where do I start?

The most important part of *tajwīd* is learning about the correct positions of the organs of speech and the manner of articulation. In other words, you must learn where the letters are supposed to come from in your mouth. The so-called difficult letters are no longer difficult if students know what to do with their lips, tongue, or throat. A pure American accent can be miraculously changed to pure, beautiful Arabic when the correct positions and manners of articulation are understood and practiced. Some students like to pass over these positions and move on to the rules of *madd* (or elongation) and the rules of the *nūn*. Yet neither of these can be done correctly if the most basic work of the *makhārij* and *ṣifāt* has not been taken care of. The Quran loses its meaning if the letters are not pronounced correctly. A very basic mistake that would be comical if it wasn't so blasphemous is the typical mistake made by many in not pronouncing the letter *qāf* correctly in the word قلب. By replacing the Arabic *qāf* with the similar but totally incorrect English letter *k*, the meaning changes from "heart" to "dog." So the reader is melodiously reciting about "your dogs" and "their dogs," and the meaning has been destroyed.

So should I stop reading the Quran until I learn all of my *makhārij*?

Definitely not! The Prophet ﷺ answered this when he said: "The one who is proficient in the recitation of the Noble Quran is associated with the honorable and obedient scribes [angels] and he who recites the Noble Quran and finds it difficult to recite, doing his best to recite it in the best way possible, will have a double reward" (*Riyāḍ al-ṣālihīn*, no. 991). In all cases, the only proven method of improvement is practice. Read with tapes, read with a teacher, read in prayer, read alone, read in groups, but read, read, read.

What if I have trouble with a letter?

First, understand exactly what your tongue is supposed to be doing. Then begin by practicing that letter alone—not in a word. For example if the difficult letter is ض, then as you learn in this book, put a *hamza* before it and a *sukūn* on it and keep trying until you get it. Once you can pronounce it alone, put it in a word like تفضيل and practice that for a while, then work on other words with different diacritical marks until the letter becomes second nature.

How can I sound like the tape I love to play?

Listen to it a lot. Practice your *makhārij*. Get the timing right—through listening and understanding and counting. Understand and practice the *ṣifāt*. The difference between a beginning student and a trained reader is only time, effort, and practice. A beautiful recitation is one that combines accurate application of the rules with a spiritually sound heart.

What about memorizing?

Read a lot while you are studying *tajwīd*, but avoid memorizing in the early stage. A verse memorized incorrectly will be doubly hard to rememorize later. As for prayer, the shorter *suwar* (the plural of sura) may be memorized from a tape in the early stages. As you improve, however, you should consistently return to the earlier memorized *suwar* to check your recitation. This is especially important as regards the Fātiḥa because its correct pronunciation is a condition of prayer. Once semiproficiency has been reached, the next step is to read through the Quran with a teacher. Once this has been accomplished, your *tajwīd* should be ready to support memorization.

What do you mean by "read through" the Quran?

The Indo-Pakistani culture has a tradition of two parties for children: one when they begin their first *khatma* and the second when it's complete. For the serious student of *tajwīd*, however, it is more complicated than just "reading through" the Quran. Each page must be meticulously practiced with a tape, listening to oneself on tape, and reading and rereading the pages until they have been perfected. Then they are read to the teacher and are corrected, and the reading continues. In this way, students learn as they read, and by the time they have finished, they are proficient and ready to memorize—or perhaps they will go further and seek out a degree in *tajwīd*.

It takes me so long to read a page because I read the translation with it. What should I do?

Try to read the Quran only in Arabic to get a feel for its rhythm and meaning without the constant interruption of English (or any second language). While there is a place for reading the translation, there is a feeling in the continuous Arabic recitation that one can experience without the constant interruption of finding out what each word means. With more involvement in the Quran, the day will come when the translation is no longer necessary. The moment when non-native students are reading and suddenly realize that they understand an entire sentence is a wonderful moment, made better because it is result of a continued connection to the Quran. As for a holistic Quranic study, time can be set aside for *tajwīd* work (when interruptions won't be allowed), and meaning work, when the focus is specific meaning and therefore the translation will be used.

What kind of *muṣḥaf* should I read from?

This is a very important question, because when the student begins to spend hours reading and reciting the Quran, the brain begins to take a picture of the pages. So that if one is constantly changing from one script to another, or from the translation to a fully Arabic *muṣḥaf*, it will be confusing and slow down the learning process. Try to choose a common script, preferably completely Arabic (no translation). The most common style now is especially designed for memorizing because the end of each page is also the end of a verse. This will be the pattern that the brain will memorize and refer back to for the rest of your life.

What else do I need to know?

All the rules of *tajwīd*—which are found on the following pages. May Allah ﷻ bless you in your reading and make the Quran the nourishment of your hearts and the light of your thoughts. May you become a walking Quran, calling others to the obedience and love of Allah ﷻ.

Biographies of Notable *Tajwīd* Scholars

Imam ʿĀṣim[2]

ʿĀṣim ibn Abī al-Nujūd (also known as Abū Bakr) was the most prominent master of recitation in Kufa. He was a *tābiʿī* (one who was a contemporary of the companions), and the *isnād* (chain of authorities) of his reading leads up to ʿAbdullāh ibn Masʿūd and ʿAlī ibn Abī Ṭālib. ʿĀṣim read to Abū ʿAbd al-Raḥmān al-Sulamī according to Ali's reading, and he read to Zirr ibn Ḥubaysh according to ʿAbdullāh ibn Masʿūd's reading. In reading to both scholars, he was fortified by combining the strongest sources (since Abū ʿAbd al-Raḥmān was a famous *tābiʿī* from whom the major imams narrated both hadith and the recitation of Quran, and Zirr ibn Ḥubaysh was a distinguished authority as well). ʿĀṣim had his student Ḥafṣ read according to ʿAlī ibn Abī Ṭālib's reading, and he had his student Abū Bakr (Shuʿba) read according to Ibn Masʿūd.

ʿĀṣim was greatly praised by scholars, and his reading was considered the first in the *mutawātir*[3] readings. He headed the reading in Kufa and had the best of voices in reading Quran. ʿĀṣim combined eloquence with *tajwīd* and perfection.

His two narrators are: Abū Bakr ibn ʿAyyāsh (Shuʿba) and Ḥafṣ ibn Sulaymān ibn al-Mughīra. Ninety five percent of the Muslims in the world today use ʿĀṣim's reading according to Ḥafṣ. ʿĀṣim died in 127 AH (may Allah have mercy on him and reward him for this *ummah*). His date of birth is unknown.

---

[2] *Muʿjam al-qirāʾāt al-Qurʾāniyya,* 1:79–80.

[3] *Tawātur*: the conveyance of a thing from one group of people to another group whereby it is impossible that they all agreed upon deception.

Imam Ḥafṣ[4]

Ḥafṣ ibn Sulaymān ibn al-Mughīra al-Dūrī al-Asadī (from the tribe of Banī Asad) (also called Abū ʿAmr) was born in 90 AH and died in 180 AH. May Allah ﷻ have mercy on him.

He was ʿĀṣim's stepson (his wife's son) and was the most knowledgeable of ʿĀṣim's reading. He moved to Baghdad and taught students how to read there. He also stayed in Mecca for a long time and taught reading there as well. He learned from ʿĀṣim how to recite the Quran correctly and how to teach reading. He reached a degree of perfection such that scholars deemed him the imam (leading scholar) of reading, and he was considered better than Abū Bakr ibn ʿAyyāsh (Shuʿba), who was the other narrator of ʿĀṣim. Ḥafṣ was famous for excellent memorization and perfection in recitation to the degree that he became generally accepted by scholars as an authority. This was as it should be considering that he was ʿĀṣim's stepson, allowing him great proximity and the closest reiteration of ʿĀṣim's reading.

Yaḥyā ibn Muʿīn said: "The correct narration of ʿĀṣim was narrated by Ḥafṣ ibn Sulaymān, because Ḥafṣ's narration goes up to ʿĀṣim ibn Abī al-Nujūd, to Abū ʿAbd al-Raḥmān ibn Ḥabīb al-Sulamī and Zirr ibn Ḥubaysh al-Asadī to ʿUthmān ibn ʿAffān and ʿAlī ibn Abū Ṭālib and ʿAbdullāh ibn Masʿūd and Ubayy ibn Kaʿb and Zayd ibn Thābit ﷺ to the Prophet to angel Jibrīl ﷺ to the Lord of Greatness ﷻ, may He be praised and His names made sacred."

Imam Shāṭibī[5]

Qāsim Abū Muḥammad al-Shāṭibī (the blind) was the most famous of those who wrote on the science of *qirāʾāt*.[6]

He was born in Shāṭiba in Andalus in 538 AH and read the different *qirāʾāt* and perfected them at the hands of Abū ʿAbdullāh ibn Muḥammad ibn al-ʿĀṣ. He traveled to Valencia in Andalus and there presented, by memory, the book *al-Taysīr fī-l-qirāʾāt al-sabʿa* ("The seven readings made easy") to Imam Abū ʿAmr al-Dānī. He presented the various readings to Ibn Hudhayl also and learned hadith from him as well.

Shāṭibī went to Egypt. There, he was warmly welcomed by Judge al-Fāḍil, given residence in the judge's school al-Fāḍiliyya, and appointed its shaykh. He taught reading and completed his famous work (*Ḥirz al-amānī wa wajh al-tahānī*), which

---

[4] *Ḥujjat al-qirāʾāt*, 59.

[5] *Sirāj al-qārīʾ al-mubtadī wa tidhkār al-muqrīʾ al-muntahī*, 3–4.

[6] *Qirāʾāt*: ways of reading the Quran.

is a compilation of what is authentic in the seven readings, in verse. This was the first rhymed work on the seven readings. Shāṭibī had memorized hadith, excelled in *qirāʾāt* (the ten readings), and was an imam of language (Arabic). He followed the Shafiʿi school of law and was known for his worship, asceticism, and leadership. He died in the year 590 AH. May Allah ﷻ have mercy on him.

Ibn Jazarī al-Dimashqī[7]

His name was Abū Khayr Muḥammad ibn Muḥammad ibn ʿAlī ibn Yūsuf, but he was known as Ibn Jazarī al-Dimashqī.

Ibn Jazarī was born in Damascus in 751 AH. He memorized the Quran perfectly when he was fourteen, then he studied hadith and the ten readings. He built a school in Damascus that he named Dār al-Qurʾān al-Karīm.

He headed the science of *iqrāʾ* (reading) in Damascus at the Umayyad Mosque, and he was appointed as a judge in Damascus in 793 AH. In 805 AH, he moved to Shiraz (Iran) with Tamerlane.

Ibn Jazarī was a prolific writer on a variety of subjects. *Al-Nashr fi-l-qirāʾāt al-ʿashr* ("On the ten readings") is the most famous of his writings. He also wrote on the subject of the ten readings in verse, which he called *Ṭayyiba al-nashr*. Also very famous is his "*Muqaddima* to what a reader of Quran must know"—a treatise on *tajwīd* in verse that became very popular among the specialists in this science. It was explained by the Shaykh of Islam, Shaykh Zakariyya al-Anṣārī, and this explanation was reviewed by Shaykh Abū Ḥasan Muḥayyiddīn al-Kurdī. Ibn Jazarī died in Shiraz in 833 AH. May Allah have ﷻ mercy on him.

[7] *Taqrīb al-nashr fī al-qirāʾāt al-ʾashr,* 5, 8.

The Science of *Tajwīd*

A Brief History

Tajwīd is a completely static science. There is no place in it for *ijtihād* (personal reasoning). Angel Jibrīl ﷺ revealed the reading, Allah ﷻ taught him, and the Prophet ﷺ received it as he heard it. He taught his companions ﷺ the Holy Quran as he received it from Jibrīl ﷺ, urging them to recite it as it was revealed. It is narrated that he ﷺ said: "Verily Allah Most High loves for the Quran to be read as it was revealed."[8]

When Islam spread to various non-Arab lands, people who were not accustomed to the Arabic letters and sounds began to learn Quran, and much error and distortion occurred. The Muslim scholars feared the perpetuation of those errors and distortions. It was at this point that some of them recorded the rules and foundations that regulate the correct pronunciation of Quran, and they named this the science of *tajwīd*.

The rules were not made up by these scholars. In fact, all they did was closely observe the perfect readers who read as they were taught by the Prophet ﷺ and record the rules by which the earlier generations read so that younger generations could follow them. In this, their mission was similar to that of the grammarians who listened to the Arabs speak and then wrote down the rules of Arabic grammar and morphology.

There is no doubt that the rules of *tajwīd* were known to the Arabs, for they used to practice *idghām*, *iqlāb*, *ikhfā'*, and *iẓhār*;[9] these rules simply took their final organized form as they relate to the proper recitation of the Quran.

[8] *Kanz al-'ummāl*, no. 3069, 1:49.

[9] *Idghām*, *iqlāb*, *ikhfā'*, and *iẓhār* are technical terms of *tajwīd* that will be explained in full in the coming pages.

These rules aided in the preserving of the book of Allah until it reached us free of change or distortion—exactly as it was revealed.

The Definition of *Tajwīd*

Linguistically: To improve.

Technically: The correct recitation of the Quran by pronouncing each letter from its correct point of articulation,[10] with its correct short vowel, and with the appropriate manners of articulation (*makhraj*, *ḥaraka*, and *ṣifa*), while at the same time ensuring the accuracy of the letter as well.[11]

Other Definitions

Makhraj al-ḥarf (the point of articulation): The correct anatomical point from which the sound of a letter is made so that it is distinct from any other.

Ṣifāt al-ḥarf (the manner of articulation):[12] The manner (or characteristic way) by which a letter is pronounced that also distinguishes it from other letters. For example: *iṭbāq*, *isti'lā'*, *takrīr*, *rakhāwa*, *qalqala*, *hams*, etc.

The Source of *Tajwīd*

The source of *tajwīd* is the mouths of shaykhs knowledgeable in the ways of the performance of correct recitation by way of *tawātur*.

Tawātur: The conveyance of information from one group of people to another group in numbers such that it is impossible that they all agreed upon a deception.

---

[10] A letter's validity is measured by that which is inherent in the letter itself (*makhraj*, *ḥaraka*, and *ṣifa*). Those aspects cannot be removed from the letter if its to keep its validity as that letter.

[11] Accuracy of the letter: A letter is accurate when the rules resulting from the manner of articulation (*ṣifa*) are applied. For example *tafkhīm* is the result of *isti'lā'* (an elevated tongue); *tarqīq* is the result of *istifāl* (a depressed tongue). And there are other rules, such as *idghām* and *iẓhār*.

[12] The technical term *ṣifa* is most often translated as "attribute." I have chosen manner of articulation on the authority of the *Cambridge Encyclopedia of Language* that describes it as "the specific process of articulation used in a sound's production." A *ṣifa* of a letter does not describe the letter more carefully (as in an attribute) but rather describes how that letter is pronounced. Thus, the term manner of articulation. Generally, in this writing, however, the Arabic will be used to avoid confusion.

Its Legal Status

There is no doubt that the **science** of *tajwīd* is *farḍ kifāya* (that is, if some people learn it, then everyone else is not held responsible). But the **practice** of *tajwīd* is a must for everyone. That is, anyone who reads Quran must read it correctly, using the rules of *tajwīd*—even if they don't know the rules from a theoretical point of view.

The proof that *tajwīd* is obligatory (*farḍ*) can be found in the Quran, hadith, and *ijmā'*:

وَرَتَّلْنَٰهُ تَرْتِيلًا

We have recited it with distinct recitation.

(al-Furqān 32)

وَرَتِّلِ ٱلْقُرْءَانَ تَرْتِيلًا

And recite the Quran with measured recitation.

(al-Muzzammil 4)

Zayd ibn Thābit ﵁ narrated that the Prophet ﷺ said: "Verily Allah loves the Quran to be read as it was revealed."[13]

The distinguished Shaykh Muḥammad Makkī Naṣr describes an *ijmā'* (or consensus) of the scholars in his book *Nihāyat al-qawl al-mufīd*: "This infallible *ummah* [which was protected from wrong] has agreed upon the fact that *tajwīd* is obligatory from the time of the Prophet ﷺ until our time. No one has ever disputed this and that is one of the strongest pieces of evidence."

Its Purpose

To protect the tongue from error in the Book of Allah ﷻ.

Its Position and Status Among the Other Sciences

It is the most honorable because it has to do with the words of Allah ﷻ.

[13] *Kanz al-'ummāl,* no. 3069, 2:49.

The Etiquette of Quran Recitation

Allah ﷻ only accepts deeds that are correct and sincere. A sincere deed is one done for Allah ﷻ alone, and a correct deed is one done according to the rules of Sharia (Islamic law). Therefore a reader should follow certain principles when reciting. The most important rules are as follows:

1. Readers must be free of that which breaks a minor ritual ablution (*wuḍū'*) and that which breaks a major ritual ablution (*ghusl*). (In other words, they must be in a state of ritual purity).
2. The place (of reading) must be legally pure (*ṭāhir*).
3. Readers should begin with *taʿawwudh* (seeking refuge in Allah from Satan), be it at the beginning of the sura or middle. This is according to Allah's ﷻ words:

   فَإِذَا قَرَأْتَ ٱلْقُرْءَانَ فَٱسْتَعِذْ بِٱللَّهِ مِنَ ٱلشَّيْطَٰنِ ٱلرَّجِيمِ

   So when you recite the Quran, seek refuge in Allah from Satan, the expelled.

   (al-Naḥl 98)

4. Readers should say "*bismillāhir Raḥmānir Raḥīm*" at the beginning of each sura, except Sūrat al-Tawba.
5. Readers should read with spiritual openness (*khushūʿ*) out of respect for the Quran. Allah ﷻ says:

   لَوْ أَنزَلْنَا هَٰذَا ٱلْقُرْءَانَ عَلَىٰ جَبَلٍ لَّرَأَيْتَهُۥ خَٰشِعًا مُّتَصَدِّعًا مِّنْ خَشْيَةِ ٱللَّهِ

   If We had sent down this Quran upon a mountain, you would have seen it humbled and breaking down from fear of Allah.

   (al-Ḥashr: 21)

6. Readers should read with thoughtfulness, reflecting on the meaning of the words.

$$أَفَلَا يَتَدَبَّرُونَ ٱلْقُرْءَانَ أَمْ عَلَىٰ قُلُوبٍ أَقْفَالُهَآ$$

Then do they not reflect on the Quran or are there
locks upon their hearts?

(Muḥammad 24)

7. Readers should beautify their voices during reading, but without pretense. Barāʾ ibn ʿĀzib 🙦 said: "The Messenger of Allah 🙦 said: 'Beautify the Quran with your voices.'"[14] And from Abū Hurayra 🙦: "He is not of us, he who doesn't recite the Quran in a melodious voice."[15] The purpose of beautifying one's voice is to facilitate the understanding of the meaning, to move anyone that might hear it, and to appreciate the beauty of the style and words. Reciting it melodiously to entertain (as a song would) is haram (forbidden). A truly beautiful and melodious recital is that which depends on correct pronunciation and perfect application of the *tajwīd* rules.

8. Readers should read the Quran in *tajwīd* and recite in the best way.

9. Readers should hold back the urge to yawn during reading until it is gone.

10. Readers should attest to the truth of Allah's 🙦 words and be witness to the call and testament of the Prophet 🙦 after they finish recitation.

11. Readers should avoid interrupting a recitation for the purpose of talking to people, except when necessary, as in answering *salām* (Islamic greeting of peace).

12. Readers should ask Allah 🙦 for His bounty when reading a verse of mercy and seek refuge with Allah 🙦 when reading verses of warning.

13. It is required of anyone who hears the Quran recited, whether from a reader (*qāriʾ*) or a radio/television/computer or other source, to listen and think about the verses. As Allah 🙦 has said:

$$وَإِذَا قُرِئَ ٱلْقُرْءَانُ فَٱسْتَمِعُوا۟ لَهُۥ وَأَنصِتُوا۟ لَعَلَّكُمْ تُرْحَمُونَ$$

So when the Quran is recited, then listen to it and pay attention
that you may receive mercy.

(al-ʿArāf 204)

---

[14] *Sunan Abī Dāwūd*, Book of Prayer, Chapter *Istiḥbāb al-tartīl fī al-qirāʾa*, no. 1468.

[15] *Ṣaḥīḥ al-Bukhārī*, Book of Tawḥīd, Chapter of Allah's saying: "Whether you hide your words or state them openly" (al-Mulk:13), 9:188.

Supplication to Begin Reading

All praise is due to Allah and peace and blessings upon our leader Prophet Muhammad and his family and those who follow his guidance.

O Allah, make great my desire for Quran, make it a light for my vision and a cure for my heart and the departure of my worry and sadness.

O Allah, adorn my tongue with it, and beautify my face by it, strengthen my body with it, and make heavy my scales with it. Grant me the best of recitation, and strengthen me to obey you by night and by day. Gather me on the day of resurrection with Prophet Muhammad, peace and blessings be upon him, and his chosen family.

الحمدُ لله ربِّ العالمين، والصَّلاةُ والسَّلامُ على سيِّدنا محمَّدٍ وآله ومن اتَّبَعَ هداه.

اللّٰهُمَّ عَظِّم رغبتي في القرآن، واجعلْهُ نوراً لِبَصري،
وشفاءً لِصَدري، وذهاباً لهمِّي وحَزَني

اللّٰهُمَّ زَيِّن به لساني، وجمِّل به وجهي، وقوِّ به جسدي، وثقِّل به
ميزاني، وارزقني حقَّ تلاوته، وقوِّني على طاعتك آناءَ اللَّيل وأطرافَ
النَّهار، واحشُرني مع النبيِّ صلَّى الله عليه وعلى آله الأخيار.

Modes of Recitation

There are three ranks or levels of recitation:

1. *Taḥqīq*: This is a precise, methodical recitation that is meticulous and heedful of the meaning. It gives each letter, in place and manner, its rightful measure (according to the rules of *tajwīd*).
2. *Ḥadr*: This is a rapid recitation with a running flow that nevertheless takes into account the rules of *tajwīd*.
3. *Tadwīr*: This describes a midway course between *taḥqīq* and *ḥadr*.

The three modes of recitation are all permitted, so that readers might choose what is most suitable and beneficial to them. They are all included in the word "*tartīl*" as it is mentioned in the Quran:

وَرَتِّلِ ٱلْقُرْءَانَ تَرْتِيلًا

And recite the Quran with measured recitation.

(al-Muzzammil 4)

Beginning Recitation

1. Seeking Refuge

It is not acceptable to begin reciting the Quran without *taʿawwudh* (to say "*aʿūdhu billāhi min ash-Shayṭān ir-rajīm*"). This is true whether the reciter will begin from the beginning of the sura or the middle of it. This is in accordance with Allah's directive:

فَإِذَا قَرَأْتَ ٱلْقُرْءَانَ فَٱسْتَعِذْ بِٱللَّهِ مِنَ ٱلشَّيْطَٰنِ ٱلرَّجِيمِ

So when you recite the Quran, seek refuge in Allah from Satan, the expelled.

(al-Naḥl 98)

Saying *taʿawwudh* before recitation is preferred (*mandūb*) according to the majority of scholars. Some scholars, however, have ruled that it is necessary (*wājib*).

a. The Meaning

To turn toward Allah ﷻ and seek shelter in Him as one turns away from the accursed Satan.

b. The Wording

أعوذُ بالله من الشيطان الرَّجيم

Aʿūdhu billāhi min ash-Shayṭān ir-rajīm

c. The Method

Readers may say it quietly[16] if they are reciting quietly or if they are alone, whether reading out loud or quietly. In prayer, it is uttered quietly, whether the prayer is audible or not. It should be said audibly if the reader will recite in front of an audience. If reciters are reciting in turn, then the first reciter should say it audibly, and the others may say it quietly.[17]

2. The *Basmala*

a. Timing

It should be uttered when the recitation begins at the beginning of a sura. If the reciter begins within the sura, then the reader may say the *basmala* after the *ta'awwudh* or confine themself to the *ta'awwudh* alone.

b. Ruling

It is obligatory in Sūrat al-Fātiḥa according to the Shafi'i school because it is considered one of its verses. It is not incorrect according to any of the scholars to begin any sura with it except for Sūrat al-Tawba. It is preferred to begin any recitation with the *basmala* even if it is within a sura because Prophet Muhammad ﷺ said, "Any task that is not initiated with *bismillāhir Raḥmānir Raḥīm* is deficient."[18]

As for Sūrat al-Tawba, it doesn't begin with the *basmala*,[19] because in the name of Allah ﷻ there is clemency and security, and "*barā'*" (the first word of the sura) means there is no clemency or safety for the *mushrikīn*.

---

[16] The quiet recitation must be heard by the one who recites it or by those nearby. As for looking at the Quran with one's eyes without labial movement, or vocalization without the articulation of each letter from its *makhraj*—that is not recitation, it is not *tilāwa*. It may be better to describe it as observation. Beware also of attempting to recite correctly in front of an imam, teacher, shaykh, or people, then leaving the application of rules and performing poorly when you are between the hands of Allah.

[17] So that as one of them finishes their recitation, the other begins where the first left off. The audible *ta'awwudh* of the first counts for the quieter ones of the rest.

[18] Imam al-Munāwī in his book *Fayḍ al-Qadīr*, no. 6284, 5:13–14. "It was related by 'Abdul Qādir al-Rahawī in the beginning of the book *The Forty Baladaniah* and it is said to be from Abū Hurayra ؓ. al-Nawawī said in *al-Adhkār* "It is a *ḥasan* hadith (of good status), and it has been related *mawsūl* (connected) and *mursal* (that which goes back to the second generation after the Prophet ﷺ). He said: The connected hadith has a good *isnād*. When a hadith is narrated *mawsūl* or *mursal*, it is considered to be connected, by the majority of scholars."

[19] Some scholars have said that the saying of the *basmala* when beginning Sūrat al-Tawba is haram (forbidden), and *makruh* (despised/hated) within the sura. Others have said that it is *makruh* (hated) upon beginning the sura and rewarded if recited within it.

How to Recite the *Basmala* Between Two Suras:

1. Complete separation: Stop at the end of the previous sura, stop after the *basmala*, and then begin the following sura.
2. Stopping after the first and connecting the second to the third: Stop at the end of the previous sura, and then connect the *basmala* to the following sura.
3. Complete connection: Connect the end of the previous sura to the *basmala* and then to the next sura. It is prohibited to connect the end of a sura with the *basmala* and then to stop.

Note: If it happens that the reciter breaks their recitation as a result of a cough, sneeze, or speech that is related to the recitation (as in explanation [*tafsīr*]) and then continues the recitation, it is not necessary to repeat the *taʿawwudh*. If the recitation is broken as a result of something foreign to the recitation, such as distraction from the recitation, unrelated talk, or food, then the *taʿawwudh* should be repeated.

The *Makhārij*

A *makhraj* is the physical place from which a letter is voiced. The different *makhārij* allow the letters to be differentiated from each other. This is true for consonants[20] and vowels.[21]

A *makhraj* can be identified by placing either a *sukūn* or a *shadda* on the letter, then preceding it with a *hamza* ء. Upon articulation, the point that the ending vocalization occurs from is the *makhraj*.

The *makhārij* can be divided into five main categories (or places), which can then be broken down into seventeen subcategories (or more specific places).

The Five Organs of Speech *al-Makhārij* are:

1. *al-Jawf,* or the internal cavity
2. *al-Ḥalq,* or the throat
3. *al-Lisān,* or the tongue
4. *al-Shafatān*, or the lips
5. *al-Khayshūm*, or the nasal cavity

---

[20] That is a *makhraj muḥaqqaq*, wherein the *makhraj* is fixed on a specific point on a part of the throat, tongue, or lips.

[21] That is a *makhraj muqaddar*, wherein the *makhraj* is not fixed on a specific point, and they are the three letters of the *madd* (elongation).

1. *al-Jawf* (The Internal Cavity)

Al-Jawf is the internal cavity, or the space that occurs after the throat and into the mouth. It is the *makhraj* of the vowel sounds, or the three *madd* (elongated) letters.

- *Alif* ا It has a *sukūn*, and the letter before it has a *fatḥa*.
- *Waw* و It has a *sukūn*, and the letter before it has a *ḍamma*.
- *Yā'* ي It has a *sukūn*, and the letter before it has a *kasra*.

These three letters are found together in His ﷻ speech:

نُوحِيهَآ[22]

They begin at the *jawf* and end with the last of the voice in the expulsed air.

2. *al-Ḥalq* (The Throat)

In the throat, there are three subcategories, which provide *makhārij* for six letters.

1. The lowest point of the throat (*aqṣā al-ḥalq*) is the place below which, the chest begins. This is the *makhraj* of the *hamza* and the *hā'*. (هـ - ء)
2. The midpoint of the throat is the *makhraj* for the *'ayn* and the *ḥā'*. (ح - ع)
3. The uppermost point of the throat is the *makhraj* for the *ghayn* and the *khā'*. (غ - خ)

[22] "Such are some of the stories of the unseen, which we have revealed unto you" (Hūd: 49).

3. *al-Lisān* (The Tongue)

The tongue has four areas, which can further be divided into ten subcategories.

a. The Furthest Point of the Tongue

It has two subcategories:

1. Where the back of the throat meets the soft area of the upper palate in the vicinity of the uvula is the point of articulation for the letter *qāf.* (ق)
2. The *makhraj* of the letter *kāf* (ك) is slightly closer to the opening of the mouth than the *qāf,* at the hard, nonfleshy part of the upper palate. It is a letter of *istifāl*—the tongue is not elevated.

b. The Middle (Blade) of the Tongue

It has a single subcategory for the three letters *jīm* (ج), *shīn* (ش), and *yā'* (ي) (but not the *yā'* of elongation).[23]

- The *jīm* is located at the point where the blade of the tongue meets the back of the alveolar ridge and the hard palate, while the front tip of the tongue is fixed at the bottom of the lower incisor teeth.
- The *shīn* and the *yā'* are located in the same area, but the tongue does not meet the alveolar ridge.

c. The Sides of the Tongue

It has two subcategories.

1. The *ḍād* (ض) is articulated at the point where one side of the tongue meets the upper molars. The left side of the tongue is most commonly used as it is easier than the right. While rare, both sides of the tongue may be used.
2. The *lām* (ل) is articulated where both sides of the tongue meet the roots of the upper front teeth.

---

[23] Note: The *yā'* other than the *yā'* of elongation is the *yā'* with a diacritical mark (a *fatḥa*, *ḍamma*, or *kasra*). Or a *yā' sākina* that is not preceded by a *kasra*.

d. The Front Tip (or Apex) of the Tongue

It has five subcategories.

1. *Nūn* – ن – The tip of the tongue also meets the upper gums. It is located slightly behind the *lām*. The nasal cavity is also involved in the final articulation of the ن. (The *makhraj* is both nasal and lingual).
2. *Rā'* – ر – Located behind the *makhraj* of the ن. This *makhraj* uses the upper side of the tongue.
3. *Ṭā', dāl,* and *tā'* – ط د ت – These letters are articulated from the base i.e. where the roots of the teeth meet the alveolar ridge. The *ṭā'* ط is the furthest from the teeth, next is the *dāl* د , and most forward is the *tā'* ت.
4. *Ṣād, sīn,* and *zay* – ز س ص – These letters are articulated from the point where the apex of the tongue meets the upper edge of the bottom of the two lower incisors. Simultaneously, air is allowed to flow from the narrow passageway between the blade of the tongue and the upper palate.
5. *Thā', dhāl, ẓā'* – ث ذ ظ – Articulated from the point where the apex of the tongue meets the edge of the upper incisor teeth.

4. *al-Shafatān* (The Lips)[24]

It has two subcategories.

1. That which is articulated when the inside of the lower lip meets the edge of the upper incisors (labio-dental). The resulting articulation is the consonant *fā'* (ف).
2. That which is articulated when both lips are used (bilabial).
   - *Waw* (أَوْ - وَ) (the nonelongated *waw*): It is articulated when the lips are rounded.
   - *Mīm* (م): Articulated by pressing the lips together and using the nasal passage.
   - *Bā'* (ب): Articulated by pressing the lips together firmly and quickly.

[24] The two sections of the lips are that which faces the inside of the mouth and that which is seen on the face. The *bā'* utilizes that which is toward the mouth; the *waw* is shaped by the outer part; and the *mīm* is between the two.

5. *al-Khayshūm* (The Nasal Cavity)

The nasal cavity is located at the furthest point of the nose. It is the opening that connects the nose and the mouth and from which the *ghunna* is articulated. The *ghunna* is a sound that is resonated; the tongue is not used to produce it. It is produced:

- When the *nūn* and/or the *mīm* has a *shadda* (is doubled).
- When the *nūn* and/or the *mīm* has a *sukūn*.
- When the *nūn* and/or the *mīm* has a *ḥaraka* (diacritical mark).
- When the *nūn* with a *sukūn* and/or the *nūn* of *tanwīn* follow the rules of *idghām*, *ikhfā'*, and *iqlāb*.
- When the *mīm* follows the rule of *idghām* as a result of another *mīm* or *ikhfā'* as a result of *bā'*.

The *Makhārij* Based on Location

1. Letters of the oral cavity (*jawfiyya*):

These are the three letters of elongation ـَ - أْ - ـُ - وْ - ـِ - يْ. They are categorized as such because they are articulated from the oral cavity, which is the open space that extends from the throat to the mouth. They are categorized as *maddiya* (elongated) because they are lengthened. They are also categorized as *hawā'iyya* because of the air that is expelled; the articulation of the letter is completed when the expulsion of air stops.

2. Letters of the throat (*ḥalqiyya*) (also guttural):

They are the *hamza, hā', 'ayn, ḥā', ghayn,* and *khā'* ء - هـ - ع - ح - غ - خ.

3. The velar letters (*lahawiyya*):

They are the *kāf* and *qāf* ك - ق. The word in Arabic is derived from *luhā* (uvula). They are called velar because their articulation takes place when the furthest point of the tongue meets the soft palate, or that place in the mouth that meets the throat.

4. The palato-alveolar letters (*shajriyya*):

They are the *jīm, shīn,* and nonelongated *yā'* ج - ش - ي. They are called palato-alveolar because they are formed at the ridge[25] of the mouth, where the middle of the tongue meets the upper palate.

[25] The ridge is that part of the upper palate that the teeth come from.

5. The flowing letters (*dhalqiyya*):

They are the *lām*, *nūn*, and *rā'* ر - ن - ل. They are called flowing letters because of the tendency of the tongue to flow towards its apex.

6. The alveolar letters (*niṭ'iyya*):

They are *tā'*, *ṭā'*, and *dāl* د - ط - ت. They are called alveolar letters because of their nearness to the alveolar area. The alveolar is that which is seen in the mouth on the upper palate. It has defining lines.

7. The apex letters (*asaliyya*):

They are the *ṣād*, *zay*, and *sīn* س - ز - ص. They are called apex letters because they are articulated from the apex of the tongue, or the point that is used for contact.

8. The interdental letters (*lithawiyya*):

They are the *thā'*, *dhāl*, and *ẓā'* ظ - ذ - ث. They are called interdental because they are articulated near the gums,[26] but not from them.

9. The labial letters (*shafawīyya*):

They are the *fā'*, nonelongated *waw*, *bā'*, and *mīm* م - ب - و - ف. They are called labial letters because they are articulated from the lips.

---

[26] The gums are the flesh surrounding the teeth in which they are rooted.

The Categories and Subdivisions of the *Makhārij*

1. *al-Jawf*: Oral Cavity (1)	
1	َ، اْ، ُ، وْ، ِ، يْ

2. *al-Ḥalq*: Throat (3)		
2	Lower	هـ، ء
3	Middle	ع، ح
4	Upper	غ، خ

3. *al-Lisān*: Tongue (10)			
Back of the tongue	5	That which follows the throat	ق
	6	Following the *makhraj* of the ق	ك
Mid Tongue	7	The nonelongated ي	ج ش ي
Side of the Tongue	8	The side of the tongue where it meets the last three molars	ض
Tip of the Tongue	9	In front of the *makhraj* of the ض	ل
	10	In front of the ل using the apex of the tongue	ن
	11	Near the *makhraj* of the ل	ر
	12	The roots of the upper teeth with the apex of the tongue	ط د ت
	13	The base of the lower teeth with the apex of the tongue	ص س ز
	14	The edges of the upper teeth with the tip of the tongue	ظ ذ ث

4. ***al-Shafatān*: The Lips (2)**			
Labial	15	The midpoint of the lower lip with the lower edge of the upper incisors	ف
		Rounded lips (nonelongated)	و
Bilabial	16	Two lips pursed together	ب
		Two lips pursed together with a *ghunna*	م

5. ***al-Khayshūm*: The Nasal Cavity (1)**		
The *ghunna*	17	*Nūn sākina* or *tanwīn* – in *idghām*
		Nūn sākina or *tanwīn* – in *ikhfā'*
		Nūn sākina or *tanwīn* – in *iqlāb*
		نّ or مّ
		مْ + م
		مْ + ب
		نْ or مْ
		Nūn and *mīm* with a *ḥaraka*

How to Pronounce...

Qalqala Letters

The letters of *qalqala* are those represented in the mnemonic device قطب جد when they are *sākina* (have a *sukūn*). They are produced when two parts of the organs of speech interact (as in the letters with a *ḥaraka*). In this case, however, the lips should not move in a way so as to produce a *fatḥa* or a *ḍamma*, nor should there be a downward movement of the lower jaw. The letter does not follow any *ḥaraka*, neither one that falls before it nor one that falls after it. This is because the letters of the *qalqala* are drawn forth just as the *ḥaraka* letters are. Thus, if it is a letter with a *shadda*, it is first firmly placed and then drawn.

For example: وتبّ - الحقّ

Mutaḥarrika Letters

These are letters that have a *fatḥa*, *ḍamma*, or *kasra* (a *ḥaraka*). (بَ ، بُ ، بِ)

This type of letter is produced when two parts of the organs of speech interact. This occurs either in the opening of the mouth, the rounding of the lips, or the downward movement of the lower jaw. It is called "the drawing forth."

Sākina Letters

1. The three letters of elongation (ـَ - ا - ـُ - وْ - ـِ - يْ).
2. The *līn* letters or diphthongs (*waw* and *yā'* when they carry a *sukūn*, and *waw* or *yā'* when the letter preceding them carries a *fatḥa*). The aforementioned are all produced by vibrating the vocal cords.

The *sākina* letters without elongation that are not the *qalqala* letters. They are produced when two parts of the organs of speech separate after firm contact. It is called "firmly placed."

Ṣifāt
(The Characteristics of Articulation)

A *ṣifa* refers to the manner of articulating the letter; a letter's *ṣifāt* differentiate it from other letters. The purpose of the *ṣifāt* is to differentiate between the letters that share articulation points (have the same *makhraj*).

There are two categories of *ṣifāt*:

1. Those that have a complement[27]
2. Those that don't have a complement

The *Ṣifāt* with Complements

There are five of these:

1. *Hams* (whispered) and *jahr* (voiced)
2. *Shidda* (plosive) and *rakhāwa* (murmured) and that which is in between, or *mutawwasiṭ* (affricate)
3. *Isti'lā'* (elevated) and *istifāl* (depressed)
4. *Iṭbāq* (closed) and *infitāḥ* (opened)
5. *Idhlāq* (flowing) and *iṣmāt* (sharply pronounced)

---

[27] The Arabic الضداد can be literally translated as "opposite." These are *ṣifāt* wherein each *ṣifa* has its opposite, or more correctly, its complement. The word complement signifies the relationship of the two *ṣifāt*, in that if a letter does not have one, then it must have the other. They complement each other.

1 _____

Hams:

<u>Linguistically</u>: Concealment.

<u>Technically</u>: The flow of breath upon pronunciation of a letter that is the result of an infirm dependency on the *makhraj*. The *hams* is evident when the letter has a *sukūn* and less so when it has a *ḥaraka*. The *makhraj* of *hams* is the same as that of the letter.

Ten letters have this attribute according to Ibn Jazarī: فَحَثَّه شَخصٌ سَكتْ

The *hams* quality remains, though to a lesser degree, when the letter does not carry a *sukūn*. In the case of the fa ف, the *hams* remains at all times. As for the *tā'* ت and *kāf* ك, the manner of articulation termed *shidda* must be considered when the letters have a *ḥaraka*. In this case, the *hams* is reduced.

The following words exemplify this rule: فِتْنَة[8] - تَتَوَفَّى[9] - شِرْكِكُم[30]

Jahr:

<u>Linguistically</u>: To proclaim.

<u>Technically</u>: Stoppage of the breath upon pronunciation of the letter as a result of the strength of application of the *makhraj*. There are nineteen *jahr* letters, which are those that do not have *hams*.

2 _____

Shidda:

<u>Linguistically</u>: Strength.

<u>Technically</u>: Stoppage of the voice upon pronunciation of the letter due to the strong reliance on, or constriction at, the point of articulation. Its letters are eight and are collected by Ibn Jazarī as follows: أَجِدْ قَطٍ بَكَتْ

Tawassuṭ: This is the *ṣifa* that lies between *shidda* and *rakhāwa* because the voice is not stopped as in the letters of *shidda*, nor continued as in the letters of *rakhāwa*. They are collected in the following: لِنْ عُمَر

Rakhāwa:

<u>Linguistically</u>: Softness/gentleness.

<u>Technically</u>: The continuation of the voice upon pronunciation of the letter. Sixteen letters are included here, those that are neither *shidda*, nor *tawassuṭ*.

---

[28] وَٱتَّقُواْ فِتْنَةً لَّا تُصِيبَنَّ ٱلَّذِينَ ظَلَمُواْ مِنكُمْ خَآصَّةً (al-Anfāl: 25)

[29] ٱلَّذِينَ تَتَوَفَّىٰهُمُ ٱلْمَلَٰٓئِكَةُ (al-Naḥl: 28)

[30] وَيَوْمَ ٱلْقِيَٰمَةِ يَكْفُرُونَ بِشِرْكِكُمْ (Fāṭir: 14)

3

Isti'lā':[31]

Linguistically: Elevation.

Technically: The elevation of the back of the tongue, upon pronunciation of a letter, to the soft palate. Its letters are seven, and they are collected by Ibn Jazarī in the following mnemonic device خُصَّ ضَغْطٍ قِظْ.

The elevation is weakened for the following letters when they have a *kasra*: *ghayn, khā', qāf* (غ، خ، ق). For example: غِض، خِلال، قِيل.

Note: The elongated *alif* follows what precedes it as to *tafkhīm* or *tarqīq*. The *ghunna* on the other hand, follows the rule of the letter that immediately follows it.

Istifāl:

Linguistically: Depressed.

Technically: The lowering or depressing of the back of the tongue away from the soft palate upon pronunciation of the letter. Its letters are all those that are not included in *isti'lā'*.

4

Iṭbāq:

Linguistically: Contact.

Technically: Contact between a part of the tongue and the upper palate upon articulation of the letter. The letters are ص ض ط ظ. This *ṣifa* is necessary for these letters even when they carry a *kasra*. The letters of *iṭbāq* are the strongest letters and have the most pronounced *tafkhīm*.

Infitāḥ:

Linguistically: Separation.

Technically: Separation or opening between the tongue and the upper palate upon pronunciation of the letter. Its letters are all except those of *iṭbāq*.

5

Idhlāq:

---

[31] As for *tafkhīm*, which is a result of *isti'lā'*, it is the thickening of the letter so that the mouth fully reverberates with its sound. It is not, however, limited to the letters of *isti'lā'* خُصَّ ضَغْطٍ قِظْ. The following letters also have the quality of *tafkhīm*: *rā'* – ر – (according to the rules that give it *tafkhīm*), *lām* – ل – (when it is found in the glorified name الله), *alif* – ا – (a *madd* letter when it is preceded by *tafkhīm*), and *ghunna* (when *tafkhīm* follows it). *Tafkhīm* is produced when at the moment of pronunciation of the letter, the back of the tongue is raised toward the upper palate.

Linguistically: Speed. The *dhalāqa* of the tongue refers to its sharpness and fluency.

Technically: The speed at which the letter is articulated from the edge of the tongue or lips upon pronunciation. It is labeled in this way because some of the letters are articulated from the edge of the tongue (*lām*, *nūn*, and *rā'* ل ن ر) and some are articulated from the lips (*fā'*, *mīm*, and *bā'* ف م ب). The letters are collected by Ibn Jazarī in the mnemonic device فِرَّ مِنْ لُبٍّ. The reciter must be aware of these so as not to enunciate so quickly that the letters are lost. This speed is evident in the following two words: أنزلْنا جعلْنا

Iṣmāt:

Linguistically: Hindrance.

Technically: Heaviness of the pronunciation of the letter. Its letters include all except for the letters of *idhlāq*. These letters are labeled as such because in the root words (whether four letters or five), it is impossible to find a word that doesn't have one or more of these letters. The Arabic language is a balanced language; the ease and lightness of the letters of *idhlāq* are balanced by the heaviness of the letters of *iṣmāt*. If at least one isn't found, then it is a word that has been adopted by the Arabs. For example, قِسْطاس, which is a scale in the language of the Romans, and found in Sūrat al-Shu'arā': 182. وَزِنُوا۟ بِٱلْقِسْطَاسِ ٱلْمُسْتَقِيمِ

Also الغَسَّاق (which is the discharge of infected wounds) and found in Sūrat al-Naba': 25. إِلَّا حَمِيمًا وَغَسَّاقًا

The *Ṣifāt* Without Complements

Ṣafīr: It is a shrillness within the sound of the letter that is produced when the sound moves through a narrow passageway. It is a sound that is similar to that of a bird and found when one of the following three letters is articulated: *ṣād, sīn, zay* ص ، س ، ز. The *ṣafīr* becomes stronger when there is a *sukūn* on the letter. For example, الوَسْواسْ.

Qalqala: (plosive/affricate): It is similar to the term staccato or an abrupt tap of one articulator against another when it has a *sukūn*, so that an audible sound occurs. A characteristic of this *ṣifa* is the quick movement of the tongue or lips upon articulation. The letters are five and are collected by Ibn Jazarī as follows: قُطْبُ جَدٍ. *Qalqala* is necessary for these letters because they have the characteristics of *jahr* (to proclaim) and *shidda* (strength). *Jahr* stops the flow of breath and *shidda* stops the flow of voice, so without the *qalqala* the sound would not be heard. There are two types:

- *Sughrā* (Minor): The letter with the *sukūn* lies in the middle of a word or the end of a word, but the recitation is not stopped at that word. For example: يطْمعون، المبْثوث، يجْعل، يدْعو، يقْطعون، لو يلدْ وَلم
- *Kubrā* (Major): The letter occurs at the end of a word and the recitation is stopped at that word. The *qalqala* is at its clearest. For example, الفلقْ، محيطْ، أحدْ، مَريجْ، قَريبْ

Līn: (diphthong): A manner of articulating that seeks an easy pronunciation. It is the *ṣifa* of three letters. The *alif* without any restrictions, and the *waw* and *yā'* when they have a *sukūn* and the letters preceding them have a *fatḥa* (not elongated). For example, خَوْف، بَيْت

Inḥirāf: The leaning of the tongue away from its *makhraj* until it nears another *makhraj*. Its letters are *lām* and *rā'* ر - ل. The *lām* leans to the apex (as opposed to the rim) of the tongue, and the *rā'* leans to the under edge of the tongue and slightly to the *makhraj* of the *lām*.

Takrīr: (flap, not trill): Only one letter is included, and it is the *rā'*. While a single tap is acceptable, the tongue should not return to the *makhraj*, because every time it does so, a *rā'* is produced. It is not acceptable for more than one *rā'* to be articulated in the position of one *rā'*.

Tafashshī: The expulsion of the air in the mouth upon pronunciation of the letter *shīn*. For example, الشَّيطان

Istiṭāla: The extension of the *makhraj* of the *ḍād* until it reaches the *makhraj* of the *lām*, utilizing the whole palate. The sound continues upon articulation as a result of its *rakhāwa*: الضَّالين

Note: All letters have five of the first category (the *ṣifāt* with complements), and may be described by one or two or none at all of the second category.

The *Ṣifāt* That Have Complements

Hams: (فَحَثَّهُ شَخْصٌ سَكَتْ) Continuation of the breath upon articulation of the letter when it has a *sukūn*.

Jahr: (the rest of the letters) Stoppage of the breath upon articulation of the letter.

Shidda: (أَجِدْ قَطٍ بَكَتْ) Stoppage of the voice upon articulation of the letter.

Tawassuṭ: (لِنْ عُمَرْ) A *ṣifa* between *shidda* and *rakhāwa*.

Rakhāwa: (the rest of the letters) Continuation of the voice upon pronunciation of the letters.

Isti'lā': (خُصَّ ضَغْطٍ قِظْ) Elevation of the back of the tongue to the soft palate.

Istifāl: (the rest of the letters) Separation of the back of the tongue from the upper palate upon articulation of the letter.

Iṭbāq: (ص ض ط ظ) Elevation of the back of the tongue to the soft palate, more so than the elevation of the remaining letters of *isti'lā'*.

Infitāḥ: (the rest of the letters) Opening of the space between the tongue and the upper palate.

Idhlāq: (فَرَّ مِنْ لُبٍّ) Speed of pronunciation of the letter from its *makhraj* whether with the tongue or lips.

Iṣmāt: (the rest of the letters) Indicates the impossibility that this type of letter alone would be found in a four or five letter root word. At least one letter or more of *idhlāq* is necessary to balance between the lightness of the *idhlāq* and the heaviness of the *iṣmāt*.

Ṣifāt: Those with Complements and Those Without

Letters	*Hams*	*Jahr*	*Shidda*	*Tawassuṭ*	*Rakhāwa*	*Isti'lā'*	*Istifāl*
ا		ج	ش				ل
ب		ج	ش				ل
ت	ه		ش				ل
ث	ه				ر		ل
ج		ج	ش	ن			ل
ح	ه				ر		ل
خ	ه				ر	س	
د		ج	ش				ل
ذ		ج			ر		ل
ر		ج		ت			ل
ز		ج			ر		ل
س	ه				ر		ل
ش	ه				ر		ل
ص	ه				ر	س	
ض		ج			ر	س	
ط		ج	ش			س	
ظ		ج			ر	س	
ع		ج		ت			ل
غ		ج			ر	س	
ف	ه				ر		ل
ق		ج	ش			س	
ك	ه		ش				ل
ل		ج		ت			ل
م		ج		ت			ل
ن		ج		ت			ل
ه	ه				ر		ل
و		ج			ر		ل
ي		ج			ر		ل

Iṭbāq	*Infitāḥ*	*Idhlāq*	*Iṣmāt*	Not paired
	ف		ص	
	ف	ذ		*Qalqala*, if it has a *sukūn*
	ف		ص	
	ف		ص	
	ف		ص	*Qalqala*, if it has a *sukūn*
	ف		ص	
	ف		ص	
	ف		ص	*Qalqala*, if it has a *sukūn*
	ف		ص	
	ف	ذ		*Inḥirāf/ takrīr*
	ف		ص	*Ṣafīr*
	ف		ص	*Ṣafīr*
	ف		ص	*Tafashshī*
ط			ص	*Ṣafīr*
ط			ص	*Istiṭāla*
ط			ص	*Qalqala*, if it has a *sukūn*
ط			ص	
	ف		ص	
	ف		ص	
	ف	ذ		
	ف		ص	*Qalqala*, if it has a *sukūn*
	ف		ص	
	ف	ذ		*Inḥirāf*
	ف	ذ		
	ف	ذ		
	ف		ص	
	ف		ص	*Līn*, if *sākina* and preceded by a *fatḥa*
	ف		ص	*Līn*, if *sākina* and preceded by a *fatḥa*

The Duration of the Letters

The Letters with a *Ḥaraka* (*Mutaḥarrika* Letters)

The duration of these letters is short and similar to each other, even when the *ṣifāt* differ. For example, the timing of ضُ and رِ and بَ is the same in the word ضُرِبَ, even though ض is a letter of *rakhāwa,* ر is a letter between *shidda* and *rakhāwa*, and ب is a letter of *shidda*.

The Letters with *Sukūn* (*Sākina* Letters)

a. Letters of Elongation

The elongated letters are prolonged by the rules of elongation.

b. Other Letters

Shidda Letters (أَجِدْ قَطٍ بَكَتْ): The duration of pronunciation of the letter is limited because the voice is cut off when the letter is pronounced. For example: يألمون . As much as one emphasizes the *hamza*, it still won't produce more sound because it is repressed.

Letters That Fall Between (لِنْ عُمَرْ): The duration of pronunciation is longer than that of the letters of *shidda*. For example: يعلمون . The voice, upon pronunciation of the ع and the ن, flows slightly.

Rakhāwa Letters (the other letters): The duration of pronunciation is longer than that of the letters that fall between. For example: الرّحمن. The voice, upon pronunciation of the ح, flows clearly.

The Rules of *Mīm* and *Nūn*

Definitions

a. *al-Ghunna*

The continuous sound that is articulated from the nasal cavity without participation of the tongue. The *ghunna* obeys what follows it as to *tafkhīm* and *tarqīq*.

There are some scholars that appraise the *ghunna* according to the number of counts. They claim that the *ghunna* should be lengthened to two counts (1, 2). The correct opinion, however, belongs to the scholars who don't appraise the *ghunna* according to counts but rather rate it according to ranks: complete, most complete, and incomplete, least complete. (See *Idghām* as Related to *Ṣifāt*.)

b. *Iẓhār*

Linguistically: Clarity.

Technically: Articulation of a letter in a clear manner without any *ghunna*.

c. *Idghām*

Linguistically: Incorporation of one thing into another thing.

Technically: Blending of a letter carrying *sukūn* into another letter carrying another mark (*mutaḥarrik*) so that the two letters become one letter with a *shadda*, of a new type that is related to the second. If the first letter is *mutaḥarrik* and the second is *mutaḥarrik*, then it is called a major *idghām*. In the Ḥafṣ recitation, this major *idghām* is found in only two words:

مَكِّنِّي ²   تَأْمَنَّا ³

Mīm and Nūn With a Shadda

A *ghunna* is necessary for the *mīm* or *nūn* that carries a *shadda*, whether it is in one word or two. For example, (الْجَنّة، أَمّا). It is not necessary for other letters that have a *shadda*, because in the Holy Quran, only the *mīm* and *nūn* with a *shadda*[34] have a complete *ghunna*.

Mīm With a Sukūn

The *mīm sākina* has three rules. Each has the word "*shafawī*" in its name because the *makhraj* of the *mīm* is between the two lips (bilabial).

1. *Idghām Shafawī* (Blending): If a *mīm* occurs after a *mīm* that has a *sukūn*, the first *mīm* is blended into the second and they merge into one *mīm* that carries a *shadda*. It is called blending of like letters with a *ghunna* (*idghām mutamāthil*). For example, لهُمْ مَا → لهمَّا

2. *Ikhfā' Shafawī* (Concealing): If a *bā'* occurs after a *mīm* that has a *sukūn*, the *mīm* is hidden by a *ghunna*: (همْ بالآخرة). Here, pressure should not be put on the lips so as to differentiate between the *ikhfā'* and the *idghām* of the lips (this is likewise noted in the case of *iqlāb*).

3. *Iẓhār Shafawī* (Clarity): If any letter other than a *mīm* or *bā'* occurs after the *mīm* with a *sukūn*, then it is necessary to clearly enunciate the *mīm* without a *ghunna*. For example, (مثلهمْ كَمَثل). This clarity of enunciation must be especially strong with the *fā'* and the *waw* to defend against their possible concealment since they originate at the same *makhraj* (the lips).

لهُمْ فيها: وَلَهُمْ فِيهَآ أَزْوَٰجٌ مُّطَهَّرَةٌۖ

أموالُكُم وَ أولادَكـم: وَٱعْلَمُوٓاْ أَنَّمَآ أَمْوَٰلُكُمْ وَأَوْلَٰدُكُمْ فِتْنَةٌ وَأَنَّ ٱللَّهَ عِندَهُۥٓ أَجْرٌ عَظِيمٌ

---

[32] Originally the first *nūn* has a *fatḥa* and the second a *kasra*. The first is blended with the second after its *fatḥa* is removed and they become one letter that carries a *shadda*. (al-Kahf 95) قَالَ مَا مَكَّنِّي فِيهِ رَبِّي خَيْرٌ

[33] Originally a *nūn* with a *ḍamma* and a *nūn* with a *fatḥa*. The first *nūn* takes on a *sukūn* then it joins the second with *ishmām*. (Yūsuf 11) قَالُواْ يَـٰٓأَبَانَا مَا لَكَ لَا تَأْمَنَّا عَلَىٰ يُوسُفَ وَإِنَّا لَهُۥ لَنَٰصِحُونَ

[34] Every *shadda* on a letter is a sign that there are two of the same letter. The first has a *sukūn* and the second is *mutaḥarrik*. The first is blended into the second and together they become one letter that carries a *shadda*.

Nūn With a *Sukūn* and *Tanwīn*

Nūn sākina: The *nūn* that carries a *sukūn* in exclusion of a *fatḥa*, *ḍamma*, or *kasra*. This is either because of original diacritical marking or as a result of stopping.

Tanwīn: A *nūn sākina* that follows a noun and is pronounced when joined with the following word. It differs in script and is not pronounced when stopped upon.

The *nūn sākina* and *tanwīn* have four rules: *iẓhār*, *idghām*, *iqlāb*, and *ikhfāʾ*.

a. *Iẓhār*

Linguistically: Clarity.

Technically: The occurrence, after a *nūn sākina* or *tanwīn*, of one of the six letters of *iẓhār*. In this case, the *nūn sākina* or *tanwīn* must be separated from the letter that follows without extending (lengthening) or elongating the *ghunna*.

Its letters: The six letters of the *makhraj al-ḥalq* (the throat): ء هـ ع ح غ خ

For example: إِنْ هُم، أَجراً حَسناً

b. *Idghām*

Linguistically: Incorporation of one thing into another.

Technically: The incorporation of the *nūn sākina* or *tanwīn* into a letter that is *mutaḥarrik* (one that is of the six letters of *idghām*) so that they become one letter with a *shadda* that is of the second type.

Thus, if, after a *nūn sākina* or a *tanwīn*, a letter of the letters of *idghām* occurs in the beginning of the next word, then the *nūn sākina* or *tanwīn* is blended into the following letter. It becomes one letter (the letter type of the new letter) with a *shadda*.[1]

Its letters: Six letters collected in the following word: يرملون

Note:

1. If a letter of *idghām* occurs after a *nūn sākina* in one word, it is not correct to treat it as *idghām*. For example, دنْيا - صِنْوان- بُنْيان - قِنْوَان
2. The *nūn* must be pronounced with *iẓhār* if a *nūn sākina* occurs at the end of a word and a *waw* occurs in the beginning of the next word in only two cases in the Quran:

(يسٓ ۝١ وَٱلْقُرْءَانِ ٱلْحَكِيمِ) is pronounced (ياسِينْ ۝١ وَٱلْقُرْءَانِ ٱلْحَكِيمِ)

(نٓ وَٱلْقَلَمِ وَمَا يَسْطُرُونَ) is pronounced (نونْ وَٱلْقَلَمِ وَمَا يَسْطُرُونَ)

3. A *tanwīn* is connected to a verb in two cases. In Sūrat Yūsuf: 32 (لَيَكُونًا) and in Sūrat al-ʿAlaq (لَنَسْفَعًا). In these cases, however, the *tanwīn* is grammatical (a *nūn* of *tawkīd* [emphasis]), so it follows the rules of *tanwīn* upon stopping. Follow the rule according to the way it is scripted in the *muṣḥaf*.

Divisions of *Idghām:*

1. *Idghām* with a *ghunna*: Its letters are four, and they are collected in the following word: يومن. For example,

   مَنْ يَعمل ← ميَّعمل

   سراجاً مُنيراً ← سراجُّمنيراً

   The *idghām* with *yā'* ي and *waw* و is called the incomplete *idghām*.
2. *Idghām* without a *ghunna*: It is called the complete *idghām*, and its letters are *lām* and *rā'*.

   يكنْ لَه ← يكلَّه

   غفورٌ رَحيم ← غفورُ رَّحيم

d. *Iqlāb*

Linguistically: Change of a thing from its original semblance.

Technically: The transformation of the *nūn sākina* or *tanwīn*, when it precedes a *bā'*, into a *mīm*. It is pronounced accordingly, taking into account the *ghunna* and the *ikhfā' shafawī*. The *mīm* that results from the meeting of a *nūn sākina* or a *tanwīn* with a *bā'* has a *ghunna* (the *ghunna* of *ikhfā'*). (Extra pressure should not be put on the lips.)

عليمٌ بذات الصدور ← عليمُمْبذات الصدور

منْ بَعد ← مِمْبَعد

e. *Ikhfā'*

Linguistically: Concealment.

Technically: Articulation of the *nūn sākina* and/or *tanwīn* in a way that is between *iẓhār* and *idghām*. It does not develop a *shadda*, but it does take on a *ghunna*. Therefore, if any letter other than those previously mentioned follows a *nūn sākina* or *tanwīn*, then the *nūn sākina* or *tanwīn* takes on an *ikhfā'* with a *ghunna*. The letters of *ikhfā'* are fifteen (all of the letters not included in the previous three rules), and they are named in the first letter of each word in the following lines of verse.

صفْ ذا ثنا كَم جَادَ شَخصٌ قَدْ سَما　　　دُمْ طَيِّباً زِدْ في تُقىً ضَعْ ظالماً

For example: يُنْفِقون

Method: When an *ikhfā'* occurs, the *makhraj* of the *nūn* or *tanwīn* is ignored and it is pronounced instead at or near the *makhraj* of the letter of *ikhfā'*. Therefore, the reader places their tongue distant from the *makhraj* of the *nūn* and close to the *makhraj* of the letter of *ikhfā'*, and performs the *ghunna*.

Note: The difference between *idghām* and *ikhfā'* is that *idghām* takes on a *shadda* and *ikhfā'* does not. Furthermore, upon *ikhfā'*, the *nūn* is hidden and all that remains is the *ghunna*.

Rules of the *Mīm Sākina*

Ikhfā' Shafawī

ب + مْ

وَهُمْ بِالآخِرَةِ

Idghām Shafawī

مْ + م

لَهُمْ مَا يَشاؤُون

(*mutamāthil, ghunna*)

Iẓhār Shafawī

any letter other than م or ب after مْ

مَثَلُهُمْ كَمَثَلِ

(مْ + other letters)

Rules of *Nūn Sākina* and *Tanwīn*

Iẓhār
with the letters of the *ḥalq*

مِنْ عَمِلٍ

مِنْ أَحَدٍ

يَنْهى

Idghām
with the letters

يرملون

Iqlāb
with *bā'* + *ghunna*

أَنْ بورك،

عليمٌ بذات الصُّدور

Ikhfā'
with other letters

مِنْ طين، سميعٌ قريب

Without *ghunna* (ل ر)

مِنْ لَدنا، مِنْ رب

With *ghunna* (ينمو)

مِنْ يقول، سراجاً منيراً

Ranking the *Ghunna*

1. **Most Complete**

   The *ghunna* is the most complete (most perfect) when the *nūn* and/or the *mīm* have a *shadda* (are stressed) and *idghām*. The most complete *ghunna* means the longest one.

   Examples: الجنَّة، خيراً يَره

2. **Complete**

   The *ghunna* is complete (shorter than the previous one) when the *nūn* or the *mīm* have *ikhfā'*.

   Examples: أنتُم، أمْ به

3. **Incomplete**

   The *ghunna* is incomplete when the *sākina nūn* or *mīm* have *iẓhār*.

   Example: أنْعَمت

4. **Most Incomplete/Least complete**

   The *ghunna* is the least complete when the *nūn* or *mīm* has a *ḥaraka*: نَ نِ نُ مَ مِ مُ

   The letters *nūn* and *mīm* cannot be without *ghunna*.

Note:

- The *makhraj* of the *nūn* has two parts. The first is lingual and becomes apparent when the tip of the tongue is firmly placed upon the alveolar ridge. The second part is nasal; the voice is emitted from the nasal cavity.
- The *makhraj* of the *mīm* has two parts: One is labial and the other is nasal.

The Rules of *Rāʾ* as They Pertain to *Tafkhīm* and *Tarqīq*

1. *Tafkhīm*

It is the elevation of the back of the tongue that produces a heavy sound.

The *rāʾ* becomes *mufakhkhama* (with *tafkhīm*) in the following situations:

1. If it has a *fatḥa* or a *ḍamma*. For example, بِرَبِّكم، رُحماء
2. If it has a *sukūn* and the letter preceding it carries a *fatḥa* or *ḍamma*. For example, زُرْتم، زَرْع
3. If it has a *sukūn* and the letter preceding it carries an original *kasra* and the letter that follows it is a letter of *istiʿlāʾ* that does not carry a *kasra* and this occurs in the same word: مِرْصَادٍ، قِرْطَاسٍ، فِرْقَةٌ، فِرْقٍ
   If, however, the letter of *istiʿlāʾ* comes in the beginning of the next word, then it has to be pronounced with *tarqīq*: فاصبِرْ صَبراً، أنذِرْ قَومك، ولا تصعِّرْ خَدّك
4. If it has a *sukūn* after an actual *hamzat waṣl*: لِمَنْ ارْتَضَى اِرجعي، أم اِرْتابوا، ارجعوا إلى أبيكم
5. If it has a *sukūn* as the result of the reciter pausing, and the letter preceding it is not a *yāʾ* and has a *sukūn*, and the letter preceding that has either a *fatḥa* or a *ḍamma*: العَصْرْ، خُسْرْ

2. *Tarqīq*

It is the depression of the back of the tongue so that a light sound is produced.

The *rā'* becomes *muraqqaqa* (in the manner of *tarqīq*) in the following situations:

1. If it carries a *kasra*: رِجَالٍ
2. If it has a *sukūn* and the letter preceding it carries an original *kasra* in the same word[35] and a letter of *isti'lā'* does not follow it: فِرْعَوْنُ
3. If it carries a *sukūn* as a result of the reciter pausing and is preceded by a *yā'* that carries a *sukūn* (elongated or otherwise): قَدِيْرْ، خَيْرْ
4. If it carries a *sukūn* as a result of the reciter pausing and the letter preceding it (a letter of *istifāl*) has a *sukūn* and the letter before that has a *kasra*: سِحْرْ

3. Optional *Tafkhīm* and *Tarqīq*

1. If the *rā'* has a *sukūn* and an original *kasra* precedes it and a letter of *isti'lā'* carrying a *kasra* follows it: فِرْقٍ
   فَٱنفَلَقَ فَكَانَ كُلُّ فِرْقٍ كَٱلطَّوْدِ ٱلْعَظِيمِ *(al-Shu'arā' 63)*
2. If the *sukūn* is a result of the reciter pausing and the letter preceding it is of *isti'lā'* and carries a *sukūn* and the letter before it carries a *kasra*: مِصْرْ
   Here, *tafkhīm* is primary because in the case of no pause (or continued recitation), it would be *mufakhkhama.*
   وَقَالَ ٱدْخُلُواْ مِصْرَ إِن شَآءَ ٱللَّهُ ءَامِنِينَ *(Yūsuf 99)*
   Whereas in the example of قِطْرْ, *tarqīq* is primary because in the case of an uninterrupted reading, it would be *muraqqaqa.*
   وَأَسَلْنَا لَهُۥ عَيْنَ ٱلْقِطْرِ *(Saba' 12)*

---

[35] Whether the *hamzat waṣl* is preceded by a helping *kasra* like أَمِ ٱرْتَابُوا or an original *kasra* as in رَبِّ ٱرْجِعُونِ *(al-Mu'minūn 99)*.

The Rules of the *Rā'*

Tafkhīm

1. If it has a *fatḥa* or a *ḍamma*: رُحَماء، بِرَبكم
2. If it has a *sukūn*, and a *fatḥa* or *ḍamma* precedes it: زَرْع، زُرْتم
3. If it has a *sukūn* and is preceded by an absolute *hamzat waṣl*: لِمَنِ ارْتضى ، اِرْجعي، أم اِرْتابوا، ارجعوا إلى أبيكم
4. If it has a *sukūn* and is preceded by an original *kasra* and followed by a letter of *isti'lā'* that has a diacritical mark other than a *kasra*: قِرْطاس، مِرْصَاد، فِرْقَة
5. If it has a *sukūn* resulting from a pause and is preceded by a *sukūn* and before that is *fatḥa* or a *ḍamma*: القَدْرْ، خُسْرْ

Tarqīq

1. If it has a *kasra*: رِزْقاً
2. If it has a *sukūn* and is preceded by an original *kasra*: فِرْعون
3. If it adopts a *sukūn* and is preceded by a *yā'* with a *sukūn*: قَديْرْ, خَيْرْ
4. If it adopts a *sukūn* as a result of a stop and is preceded by a letter of *istifāl* that has a *sukūn* and is preceded by a *kasra*: السِحْرْ

Optional *Tafkhīm* and *Tarqīq*

1. If it has a *sukūn* and is preceded by an original *kasra* and followed by a letter of *isti'lā'* that has a *kasra*: فِرْقٍ
2. If it adopts a *sukūn* at the end of the word and is preceded by a letter of *isti'lā'* that has a *sukūn* and this is preceded by a *kasra*: مِصْرْ, قِطْرْ

The Rules of *Lām* in the Name of Allah Pertaining to *Tafkhīm* and *Tarqīq*

1. *Tafkhīm*

Tafkhīm is the elevation of the back of the tongue; it produces a heavy sound. The *lām* takes on *tafkhīm* in the following situations:

1. The *lām* in the pronunciation of the name of Allah ﷻ when preceded by a *fatḥa* or a *ḍamma*, as in: قَالَ اللّٰه، قَامَ عبدُ اللّٰهِ
2. The *lām* in the utterance of His glorified name when preceded by a *sukūn* before which is a *fatḥa* or a *ḍamma* as in: إلى اللّٰه، قالُو اللّٰهم

2. *Tarqīq*

The *lām* has *tarqīq* in the following situations:

1. The *lām* in the utterance of His glorious name when preceded by an original *kasra* or a helping *kasra*: بِاللّٰه، قلِ اللّٰهم، قوماً اللّٰه ← قومنِ اللّٰه
2. The *lām* in the utterance of the most glorious name if it is preceded by a *sukūn*, and the *sukūn* is preceded by a *kasra*: يُنَجِّي اللّٰه

The Rules of the Definitive Article *Lām* as it Relates to *Idghām* and *Iẓhār*

Definition

It is a *lām sākina* that is superfluous to the conjugation of the word. It is preceded by a connecting *hamza* and a *fatḥa*, and the type of word that follows it is a noun.

Rules

a. *Iẓhār*

The definitive article *lām* is clearly pronounced when the first letter of the noun following it is a *qamariyya* letter. These letters are collected in the following: ابْغِ حَجَّكَ و خَفْ عَقِيمَه. They are called *qamariyya* letters because if a definite article occurs with the word "*qamar*," it would be clearly pronounced: "*al-qamar*." The lam, when it precedes a *qamariyya* letter, is pronounced without difficulty. When it precedes a *jīm*, however, it can sometimes lead to mistakes. So it is necessary in this case to carefully and clearly pronounce the *lām*, so that it is not lost in the *jīm*. For example, الجَنَّة

b. *Idghām*

The definite article is blended with the letter that follows it when that letter is a *shamsiyya* letter. These letters include all letters other than the *qamariyya* letters. This letter becomes stressed. They are called the *shamsiyya* letters because the *lām* is blended into the letter as it is in the word الشَّمس "*ash-shams*." The *shamsiyya* letters are all of the first letters in the following line of poetry:

طِبْ ثمَّ صِلْ رَحماً تَفُزْ ضِفْ ذا نِعَمْ　　　دَعْ سوءَ ظَنّ زُرْ شَريفاً لِلْكَرَمْ

Examples: الطَّامَّة، السَّماء، الصَّلاة

Note: The *lām* that occurs in the conjunctions الَّتي and الَّذي and the *lām* in the utterance of the name Allah ﷻ are not described as *qamariyya* or *shamsiyya* because they are part of the original conjugation of the word.

The Rules of the *Lām* When It Occurs in a Verb

Definition

It is a *lām* with a *sukūn* that is part of the conjugation of the word.

Rules

a. *Idghām*

If a *lām* or *rā'* follows it:

قُلْ رَبِّ ← قُرَّبِّ

قُلْ لاَ أملك ← قُـ أملك

b. *Iẓhār*

If any other letter occurs after the *lām*.

قُلْ يَقَوْمِ *(al-An'ām 135)*

قُلْ جَاءَ الْحَقُّ *(Saba 49)*

It is necessary to clearly pronounce this *lām* when it is followed by a *nūn* and to be sure not to blend them together because their points of articulation are near to each other: قُلْنا، جعلْنا، أنزلْنا

Idghām as Related to *Ṣifāt*

The *idghām* is divided into three categories: *mutamāthil* (of like nature), *mutajānis* (similar), and *mutaqārib* (proximate).

a. *Idghām Mutamāthil*

Mutamāthil means "of like nature." It is an *idghām* between two letters that are alike according to both their *makhraj* and *ṣifa*. The first is *sākin* and the second is *mutaḥarrik*, so that the first is blended into the second, whether in one word or two.

In one word: يُكْرِهْهُنَّ ← يُكْرِهُّنَّ

In two words: رَبِحَتْ تِجَارَتُهُم ← رَبِحَتِّجَرَتُهُم

Comments

1. The elongated *yā'* does not blend with the nonelongated *yā'*. Nor does an elongated *waw* blend with a nonelongated *waw*, because they are not of the same *makhraj*. For example:

   ٱلَّذِي يُوَسْوِسُ

   ءَامَنُواْ وَعَمِلُواْ

   The *yā'* that is not elongated, however, does blend with its counterpart as does the nonelongated *waw*, because in this case they have the same *makhraj*. For example:

   آوَوْا وَنَصَروا ← آوَوَّنَصَروا

2. *Idghām mutamāthil* does not take a *ghunna* except in two cases: a *mīm* with a *mīm* (*idghām mutamāthil shafawī*) and a *nūn* with a *nūn* (*idghām* with a *ghunna*).

3. In the words of Allah ﷻ in *(al-Ḥāqqa 28–29)*

   مَآ أَغْنَىٰ عَنِّي مَالِيَهْۜ ۝٢٨ هَلَكَ عَنِّي سُلْطَٰنِيَهْ ۝٢٩

The word مَالِيَهْ includes an additional ه (this is the *hā'* that occurs after a *yā'* ي that signifies possession), which is followed by a *hā' mutaḥarrik* هلك. In this case, it is acceptable to do *idghām*:

مَالِيَهْ هَلَك ← ماليَهَّاك

It is also acceptable to do *iẓhār* (making the *hā'* clear) مَالِيَهْ using *hams* and to separate it from the word that follows it with a short pause مَالِيَهْ هَلَك. *Iẓhār* is more common.

b. *Idghām Mutajānis*

When two similar letters of like *makhraj* and different *ṣifa* follow one another, the first is *sākin* and the second is *mutaḥarrik*. The first is blended into the second, and they are of three points of articulation:

Makhraj of the *ṭā'* and the *tā'* and the *dāl* د، ت، ط

An *idghām* is necessary in the following instances:

1. The *dāl* (د) blended into the *tā'* (ت):

   قدْ تبين ← قتّبين (al-Baqara 256)

2. The *tā'* (ت) blended into the *dāl* (د):

   أُجِيبتْ دَعوَتُكما ← أُجيبدَّعْوَتُكما (Yūnus 89)

3. The *tā'* (ت) blended into the *ṭā'* (ط):

   همَّتْ طائفتان ← همَّطّائفتان (Yūnus 89)

4. The *ṭā'* (ط) blended into the *tā'* (ت)

   أحطتُ (al-Maida 28)، بَسَطتَ (al-Naml 22)

The *ṭā'* ط in the case of (أحطتُ، بسطت) has the *ṣifa* of *iṭbāq* and *qalqala*. With the *idghām*, the *ṣifa* of *qalqala* is eliminated, but the *ṣifa* of *iṭbāq* remains. It remains because the letter *ṭā'* (ط) is stronger than *tā'* (ت). In this case, it is considered an incomplete *idghām*.[36]

[36] The difference between the complete *idghām* and the incomplete *idghām* is that in an incomplete *idghām*, the *ṣifa* of the blended letter remains, whether it is *iṭbāq* أحطت or *isti'lā'* نخلقكم or a *ghunna* من يعمل. The complete *idghām* is when nothing of the blended letter remains, and that is because its *ṣifa* has blended into the next letter.

Makhraj of the *ẓā'*, *dhāl*, and *thā'* ظ ذ ث

The *idghām* is necessary in two instances.

1. The *dhāl* (ذ) blended into the *ẓā'* (ظ):
   إِذْ ظَلموا ← إظَّلموا *(al-Nisā' 64)*
2. The *thā'* (ث) blended into the *dhāl* (ذ):
   يَلْهَثْ ذَلك ← يَلْهَذَّلك *(al-'Arāf 176)*

Makhraj of the *mīm* and *bā'* م ب

Idghām is necessary in one instance: The *bā'* as it is blended into the *mīm*: اركَبْ مَعَنا ← ار كَمّعنا *(Hūd 42)*

c. *Idghām Mutaqārib*

Two letters have a *makhraj* or *ṣifa* with close proximity. Proximity of the *makhraj* means that there are two letters from the same area but they differ in exact point. For example, the last part of the throat and the midpoint of the throat. Proximity of the *ṣifa* means that the letters share more than one *ṣifa*. In the case of two letters with proximity, the first is blended into the second.

Idghām is necessary in the following two cases:

1. *Lām* (ل) into *rā'* (ر):
   بَلْ رَفعه ← بَرَّفعه *(al-Nisā' 158)* وقل رَب ← وقرَّبِّ *(Ṭāhā 114)*
2. *Qāf* (ق) into *kāf* (ك): أَلَمْ نَخْلُقكُّم *(al-Mursalāt 20)*

If the *qāf* is blended into the *kāf* completely, it becomes a pure *kāf* with a *shadda* and as in نخلكُّم, there is a complete *idghām*. This is used more often. It can also be pronounced with *isti'lā'* for the *qāf* remaining. This is used less often. Both are correct.

Idghām as Related to *Ṣifāt*

Mutamāthil

The blending of a letter that carries a *sukūn* with another letter like it that is *mutaḥarrik* so that they become one letter with a *shadda*. This may occur in one word or two.

ربحتْ تِجارَتُهم ← رَبِحتّجترَتُهم
يُكْرِهْهُنّ ← يُكْرِهُنّ
آوَوْا وَنَصروا ← آوَوّنَصروا
اتّقَوْا وآمنوا ← اتّقَوّا منوا

Since they don't have the same *makhraj*, the elongated *yā'* does not become blended with another nonelongated *yā'* and neither does an elongated *waw* become blended with a nonelongated *waw*.

ال ذي يَتسن، الذي يُوسوس، آمنوا وَعملوا

Idghām mutamāthil does not take a *ghunna* except in two cases:

1. *Mīm* into a *mīm* (*idghām shafawī*) مِنْهُمْ من ← منهمّن
2. *Nūn* into a *nūn* (*idghām* with a *ghunna*) مِنْ نَار ← منّار

Mutajānis

The blending of a letter that has a *sukūn* with one that is *mutaḥarrik* and similar in pronunciation because it is from the same area of articulation.

1. *Makhraj* of the (ط) and (ت) and (د):
   a. *Dāl* (د) into *tā'* (ت): قَدْ تبين ← قتّبين
   b. *Tā'* (ت) into *dāl* (د): أجيبت دعوتكما ← أجيبدّعوتكما
   c. *Tā'* (ت) into *ṭā'* (ط): هَمّتْ طَائفتان ← همّطّائفتان
   d. *Ṭā'* (ط) into *tā'* (ت): بسطتَ
2. *Makhraj* of the (ظ) and (ذ) and (ث). *Idghām* is necessary in two cases:
   a. *Dhāl* into *ẓā'*: إذْ ظَلمتم ← إظّلمتم
   b. *Thā'* into *dhāl*: يلهثْ ذَلك ← يلهذّلك
3. *Makhraj* of *mīm* and *bā'*. *Idghām* is necessary in one case:
   Blending of the *bā'* into the *mīm* اركبْ مَعنا ← ار كمّعنا

Mutaqārib

The blending of a letter into a letter that is in proximity to it by *makhraj* and *ṣifa*. *Idghām* is necessary in two instances:

1. *Lām* (ل) into *rā'* (ر):

وقُلْ رَبِّ ← وقرَّبِّ

2. *Qāf* (ق) into *kāf* (ك):

    نَخْلُقْكُم

    a. Complete *idghām:* نخلقكم

    b. Incomplete *idghām:* نخلكُّم

The Rules of *Madd* (Elongation)

Definitions

a. *Madd*

Linguistically: (زيادة) To lengthen, elongate, draw out.

Technically: Lengthening of the sound of a letter of elongation (*alif sākina* preceded by a *fatḥa*, *waw sākina* preceded by a *ḍamma*, *yā' sākina* preceded by a *kasra*), or a letter of the two letters of *līn*. The letters of *madd* are three, collected in the word نُوحِيهَا from the verse in the Quran:

تِلْكَ مِنْ أَنۢبَآءِ ٱلْغَيْبِ نُوحِيهَآ إِلَيْكَ *(Hud 49)*

b. *Qaṣr*

Qaṣr means "shortening," and it refers to limiting an elongated letter to only two counts.

Types of *Madd*

1. The Original *Madd* (*Madd Aṣlī*)
2. The Derived *Madd* (*Madd Far'ī*)
3. Exceptional *Madds* (accompanying or appended to either of the preceding types)

1. *Madd Aṣlī*

It is called the natural *madd* (*madd ṭabī'ī*). There is no external reason for this *madd*; the letter itself is simply incorrect without it. It is called natural *madd* because it is natural and smooth and isn't longer or shorter than two counts. Two counts is the amount of time it would take to say two letters immediately following each other. For example, قَ قَ, or to pronounce the letter *alif* in the word قال by a normal healthy person.

A derivative of *madd ṭabīʿī* is *Madd Tamkin*. It is the elongation of the *yāʾ* that occurs after a *yāʾ* with a *shadda* and a *kasra*. It is to emphasize the *shadda* and to clarify the elongation.

حُيِّيتم، النَّبِيِّين

It is forbidden to lengthen or shorten natural *madd* to become more or less than two counts.

2. *Madd Farʿī*

The cause of the lengthening is external and is either due to a *hamza* or a *sukūn*.

<u>*Madd* Caused by a *Hamza*</u>

1. ***Madd Muttaṣil Wājib***

   This refers to the occurrence of a letter of *madd* followed by a *hamza* in a single word. In Ḥafṣ, it is lengthened according to the way of Shāṭibiyya, which is four or five counts.

   However, if the *hamza* is the last letter, and the reader stops at it, then it is lengthened to four or five or six counts.[37]

   For example, يتسَاءلون ، سِيئَت، شَاءْ

   It is called *wājib* (necessary) because of the agreement of the reciters on the necessity of elongation for a longer period than that of *madd ṭabīʿī*. It is called *muttaṣil* (connected) because the *hamza* and the *madd* are found in one word.

2. ***Madd Munfaṣil Jāʾiz***

   This refers to the occurrence of a letter of *madd* at the end of a word, which is followed by a word whose first letter is a *hamza*. In Ḥafṣ, it is lengthened to four or five counts according to the way of Shāṭibiyya, and it is possible to shorten it to the length of a *madd ṭabīʿī*. (This is the way of Ṭayyibat al-Nashr.) For example, يا أيُّها

   It is called the separated *madd* (*munfaṣil*) because of the separation of the *madd* letter and the *hamza* into two words. It is called permissible (*jāʾiz*) because of the possibility of shortening or lengthening.

[37] The connected *madd muttaṣil* in the Shāṭibiyya way is elongated only four or five counts, but if the *hamza* is the last letter and the reader stops at it, then it is lengthened to six counts because of the *sukūn*, which is the reason for having *madd ʿāriḍ li-l-sukūn* (influenced by a stop), not because of the *madd muttaṣil* (connected elongation).

<u>*Madd* Caused by a *Sukūn*</u>

1. ***Madd ʿĀriḍ li-l-Sukūn***

   When a temporary *sukūn* follows a letter as a result of a stop or pause in recitation, then an *ʿāriḍ madd* occurs. For example:

   عِقاب، نستعين، مُفلحون

   It is acceptable to shorten it to *al-qaṣr* (two counts) or extend it to mid-length (four counts) or further extend it to a prolonged length (six counts). It is preferred to draw it out to four or six counts.

2. ***Madd Lāzim***

   When an original *sukūn* or a letter with a *shadda* follows a *madd* letter (because a letter with a *shadda* is originally two letters that are the same, the first of which is *sākin* and the second of which is *mutaḥarrik*). It has been uniformly agreed that its length is six counts. There are two types: *kalimī* and *ḥarfī* (words and letters).

   a. Madd Lāzim <u>Kalimī:</u>

   It occurs in a word.

   It is called *muthaqqal* (heavy) when a letter with a *shadda* follows a *madd* letter. For example: (الضَّالِّين، أتحاجُّنِّي، الحاقَّة، آلذَّكَرَيْن، آالله، تأمرونِّي)

   It is called *mukhaffaf* (lightened) if the *madd* letter precedes a letter that has an original *sukūn* without a *shadda*. For example:

   (آلآنَ) is (أَاالآنَ)

   The second *hamza* was exchanged for a *madd* letter and so it became necessary to lengthen it to six counts.

   It is acceptable to reduce the second *hamza* instead of replacing it. In this case, it would be read between the *hamza* and the *alif*, and it would not be lengthened.

   b. Madd <u>al-Farq</u>

   This is actually a *madd lāzim kalimī*, but it is called *farq* because it differentiates between statement and question indicators. This *madd* is found between the first *hamza* and the second, which is part of the first word of the statement. If a *hamza* that indicates a question precedes the *hamzat waṣl* of the utterance of His glorified name or a noun with a definite article, then the second *hamza* is exchanged for an *alif* and it is lengthened to six counts.

This occurs in three words in the Holy Quran in six instances:

ءَآللهُ آللهُ:

قُلْ ءَآللَّهُ أَذِنَ لَكُمْ *(Yūnus 59)*

ءَآللَّهُ خَيْرٌ أَمَّا يُشْرِكُونَ *(al-Naml 59)*

آلذَّكَرِين ءَآلذَّكَرَيْنِ:

قُلْ ءَآلذَّكَرَيْنِ حَرَّمَ أَمِ ٱلْأُنثَيَيْنِ *(al-Anʿām 143–144)*

ءَآلْـٰـنَ آلآنَ:

ءَآلْـٰـنَ وَقَدْ كُنتُم بِهِۦ تَسْتَعْجِلُونَ *(Yūnus 51)*

ءَآلْـٰـنَ وَقَدْ عَصَيْتَ *(Yūnus 9)*

c. Madd Lāzim Ḥarfī

It occurs in the letters that are found in the opening verse of various suras. They are spelled with three letters, of which the middle letters are either *madd* letters or *līn* and those letters are brought together in the following saying (نقُص عَسَلُكُم). It is called *muthaqqal* (heavy) if an *idghām* follows it: طسٓمٓ لٓمٓر الٓم

It is called *mukhaffaf* if the letter that follows the *madd* letter carries a *sukūn* and does not take on an *idghām* with the letters that follow it. It is lengthened to six counts. For example: صٓ *(Ṣād 1)*

As for the letter that has a diphthong (*līn*), as in the spelling of the letter ع, according to Shāṭibiyya, it is lengthened to four or six counts.[38] Imam Shāṭibī said: "The ع has two possible pronunciations, and the longer is preferred." Thus a mid-length or a protracted length is preferred. It is lengthened two counts in the way of Ṭayyiba. It occurs in the Quran: حمٓ عٓسٓقٓ كٓهيعٓصٓ

As for letters spelled with two letters that occur in the opening verses of some suras, they are: (حَيٌّ طَهُر). They are lengthened two counts according to their original spelling, which includes a *madd ṭabīʿī*.

(حا، يا، طا، ها، را)

Further, one letter that does not take a *madd* at all is *alif*, and that is because it has no *madd* letters in its spelling.

---

[38] As it is related to *madd līn*.

Note:

In the Holy Quran, there are:

- Three suras that open with single letters: (ص، ق، ن)
- Ten suras that open with two letters:
  Seven with: (حم), one of which also has (عسق) *(al-Shūrā)*
  Three that begin with: (طه، طس، يس)
- Thirteen suras that open with three letters:
  Six arranged as: (الم)
  Five arranged as: (الر)
  Two arranged as: (طسم)
- Two suras begin with four letters: (المص، المر)
- One sura with five letters (كهيعص)

3. Exceptional *Madds*

Ṣila Madd: It connects the *hā'* masculine pronoun[39] (the *hā'* as it occurs as a pronoun to designate a single male who is absent) with the *madd* letter that relates to the diacritical mark (*ḥaraka*) of the letter if this *hā'* lies between two letters that are both *mutaḥarrik*. There are two types:

1. **Major Ṣila (Kubrā):** If a *hamza* occurs after the pronoun *hā'*, then the *hā'* extends to the *madd* letter that is related to its *ḥaraka*. Then it adopts the rule of the *madd munfaṣil* so that it is lengthened to two or four or five counts according to how long the reciter lengthens the *madd munfaṣil*.
   مَالَهُۥٓ أَخْلَدَهُۥ ← ماله‍و أخلده *(al-Humaza 3)*
   وَمِنْ ءَايَـٰتِهِۦٓ أَنْ خَلَقَكُم مِّن تُرَابٍ ← ومن آياته‍ي أنْ خلقكم من تراب *(al-Rūm 20)*
   Note: Reciters must ensure that their lengthening counts are consistent from the beginning of their reading to the end.
2. **Minor Ṣila (Sughrā):** If a letter other than *hamza* occurs after the pronoun *hā'*, then the *hā'* lengthens to the *madd* related to its *ḥaraka*. It then follows the rule of *madd ṭabīʿī* and must be lengthened to two counts.
   إِنَّهُۥ بِعِبَادِهِۦ خَبِيرٌۢ بَصِيرٌ ← إنّهو بعباده‍ي خبير *(al-Shūrā 27)*

[39] The *hā'* feminine pronoun of the demonstrative pronoun *hadhihi* (هذه) is treated as the *hā'* masculine pronoun, without any addition or diminution.

There are a few exceptions that do not follow the rules of *madd ṣila.*

فيْهِ مُهانا: Ḥafṣ lengthens it even though the letter preceding the *hā'* carries a *sukūn:* وَيَخْلُدْ فِيهِۦ مُهَانًا → فيهي مهانا *(al-Furqān 69)*

يرضه: The *hā'* is not elongated even though it is between two letters that are *mutaḥarrik:*

وَإِن تَشْكُرُواْ يَرْضَهُ لَكُمْ ← إن تشكروا يرضهُ لكم *(al-Zumar 7)*

Note:

Ḥafṣ reads فَأَلقِهْ إليهم with a *sukūn* on the *hā'* *(al-Naml 28).*

Ḥafṣ reads أَرجِهْ و أخاه with the omission of the *hamza* and a *sukūn* on the *hā'* *(al-Shu'arā' 36 and al-'Arāf 111).*

Madd Badal: Every lengthened *hamza* (every *hamza* followed by a *madd* letter in one word) is lengthened to two counts. There are two types:

1. **Original *Madd Badal*:** When a *madd* letter is exchanged for the *hamza*, then the rule for an exchange is applied. If two *hamzas* occur one after the other in the same word and the first is *mutaḥarrik* and the second is *sākin*, then the second *hamza* is exchanged for the *madd* letter that is related to the *ḥaraka* of the first. For example:

   إيمان is إِإْمان
   أوتوا is أُأْتُوا
   آدم is أَأْدَم
   ايذن is اِئذن
   اؤتمن is أُؤْتمن

2. ***Madd* That Is Like the *Badal*:** When that which follows the *hamza* is not a *madd* letter exchanged for a *hamza*. The length of this *madd*, according to Ḥafṣ by Shāṭibiyya, is two counts. For example:

   يؤوس، تشاءون، مآب

Madd 'Iwaḍ: This is an elongation that occurs when the reader stops, in place of the *tanwīn* that sits atop an *alif* in a continued reading. It is elongated as a *madd ṭabī'ī*. For example, رحيمًا ← رحيمَا However, if the last letter of a word is a *tā' marbūṭa* (ة), then it is stopped upon as a *hā' sākina* and carries the *ṣifa hams:* فتنةً ← فتنهْ

<u>*Madd Līn:*</u> The *madd* of the two diphthong letters *waw* and *yā’* when they carry a *sukūn* and the letter preceding them carries a *fatḥa* and the letter following them carries a *sukūn*, as a result of stopping. It is permissible to lengthen as *qaṣr*, mid-length, or prolonged (two, four, or six counts).

خَوْفْ، قُرَيْشْ

Note: The pronunciation of the *madd* letters (*alif, yā’, waw*) is omitted at the end of a word only for the purpose of connecting if the letter that follows them (in the root word) is *sākin*.

1. *Alif* at the end of the word:

    (*al-Nisā’ 176*) فَإِن كَانَتَا ٱثۡنَتَيۡنِ ← فإن كانتَ اثنتين

    (*al-‘Arāf 22*) فَلَمَّا ذَاقَا ٱلشَّجَرَةَ ← فلمَّا ذاقَ الشَّجرة

    (*Yūsuf 25*) وَٱسۡتَبَقَا ٱلۡبَابَ ← واستبقَ الباب

    (*al-Naml 15*) وَقَالَا ٱلۡحَمۡدُ لِلَّهِ ← وقالَ الحمد الله[40]

2. *Waw* at the end of the word:

    (*Ṣād 59*) إِنَّهُمۡ صَالُواْ ٱلنَّارِ ← إنَّهم صالُ النَّار

    (*Yāsīn 59*) وَٱمۡتَٰزُواْ ٱلۡيَوۡمَ ← وامتازُ اليوم

    (*al-An‘ām 108*) وَلَا تَسُبُّواْ ٱلَّذِينَ ← ولا تَسبُّ الذين

3. *Yā’* at the end of the word:

    (*al-Mā’ida 1*) مُحِلِّي ٱلصَّيۡدِ ← مُحِلِّ الصَّيد

    (*al-Ḥajj 35*) وَٱلۡمُقِيمِي ٱلصَّلَوٰةِ ← و المُقيمِ الصَّلاة

    (*al-Zumar 61*) وَيُنَجِّي ٱللَّهُ ← و يُنجِّ اللَّه

---

[40] *Al-Nabr* النبر should be used in the words (واستبقا - وقالا - ذاقا) to avoid confusion between the dual tense and the singular form. *Al-Nabr* is pressure on a syllable or a specific letter in a word so that the volume is raised in comparison to the surrounding letter and the syllables of that word.

Types of *Mudūd*

A. Not *Ṭabīʿī*

1. Caused by a *Sukūn*

   a. Lāzim: Caused by an original *sukūn* that occurs after a *madd* letter, requiring six counts.

   i. Ḥarfī: A *sukūn* that occurs after a *madd* letter in the spelling of the letter.

   1. Heavy: A three letter spelling where the final letter blends with the letter that follows: الم المر طسم
   2. Light: A three letter spelling the final letter does not blend with the letter that follows it: قاف ميم

   ii. Kalimī: A *sukūn* that occurs after a *madd* letter in a word.

   1. Heavy: A *madd* letter followed by a letter with a *shadda*. الحاقّة
   2. Light: A *madd* letter followed by a letter with a *sukūn*. آلآنْ

   b. ʿĀriḍ li-l-sukūn: Caused by a *sukūn* that is not original to the word but is caused by a stop and occurs after a *madd* letter. Two, four, or six counts.

2. Caused by a *Hamza*

   a. Wājib Muttaṣil: Four or five counts جاء، ملائكة، سوء

   b. Jā'iz Munfaṣil: Two, four, or five counts إنا أنزلناه

B. *Ṭabīʿī*

The letters ا، و، ي have two counts. They are found in the word نُوْحِيْهَا.

Notes:

The order of strength of the *mudūd* is *lāzim, muttaṣil, ʿāriḍ li-l-sukūn, munfaṣil, badal.*

If two causes for *madd* occur together, the stronger is chosen. For example: الدعاء when stopped upon has two causes for *madd*. The first is *ʿāriḍ li-l-sukūn* and the second is *muttaṣil*. So follow that which is stronger. It is impossible in this case that it would only have two counts.

Branches of *Madd*

1. *Madd Ṣila*
    a. Minor *Ṣila Madd*: When the masculine pronoun *hā'* (ـه) falls between two letters that both have a *ḥaraka* and the following letter is not a *hamza*. For example: إِنَّهُ هو. It has two counts.
    b. Major *Ṣila Madd*: When the masculine pronoun *hā'* (ـه) falls between two letters that both have a *ḥaraka* and the following letter has a *hamza*. For example: ولَهُ أَجر. Its length is two, four, or five counts, according to its relationship to *madd munfaṣil*.
2. *Madd 'Iwaḍ*: A *madd* that occurs only upon stopping at a word that has an *alif* with a *tanwīn*. For example: عليماً ← عليما. It has 2 counts.
3. *Madd Līn*: Occurs in the case of a *waw sākina* or a *yā' sākina* when the letter before has a *fatḥa* and the following letter has a *sukūn* as the result of a stop. خَوْف، بَيْت Its length is two, four, or six counts.
4. *Madd Badal*: A *hamza* precedes a *madd* letter in one word.

    For example: أوتوا إيمان

    It has two counts.

Exceptions:

- The only word where the masculine pronoun *hā'* is elongated even though the letter before it does not have a *ḥaraka* is the word فيه, as is found in His words in Sūrat al-Furqān: 69 (ويخلد فِيْه مهاناً). In other words, the *hā'* is elongated in spite of the fact that the letter before it is *sakin*.
- Exempted from the *ṣila* rule is the masculine pronoun *hā'* in His words in Sūrat al-Zumar: 7 (وإن تشكروا يرضَهُ لَكم). In other words, the *hā'* in يرضه is not elongated even though it is between two letters that are *mutaḥarrika*.
- Ḥafṣ reads Sūrat al-Naml: 28 with a *sukūn* on the ha: (فألقِهْ إليهم)
- Ḥafṣ reads Sūrat al-'Arāf: 111 and Sūrat al-Shu'arā': 36 by omitting the *hamza* and with a *sukūn* on the ha: (أرجه و أخاه). Its original form is أرجئه.

The Seven *Alifs*

The following *alifs* are pronounced upon stopping and omitted during continuous recitation:

1. *Alif* in (أنا): Personal pronoun referring to "I." Its pronunciation is omitted upon continuous recitation throughout the Quran.
2. *Alif* in (لكنَّاْ) in Sūrat al-Kahf[41]
3. *Alif* in (الظُّنوناْ) in Sūrat al-Aḥzāb[42]
4. *Alif* in (الرَّسولاْ) in Sūrat al-Aḥzāb[43]
5. *Alif* in (السَّبيلاْ) in Sūrat al-Aḥzāb[44]
6. *Alif* in (قواريراْ) in Sūrat al-Dahr[45]
7. *Alif* in (سلاسلاْ) in Sūrat al-Dahr[46]

   It is permissible in the case of stopping on the word (سلاسلا) to stop on the *lām*, which then takes on a *sukūn*. Omit the *alif/madd* and say (سلاسلْ).

   Thus, there are two possibilities in the case of stopping:

   - To stop at the *lām sākina* without an *alif* after it: سلاسلْ
   - To stop on the *alif* after the *lām*: سلاسلا

   In the case of not stopping, the words are read سلاسلَ و أغلالاً

41 لَّٰكِنَّا۠ هُوَ ٱللَّهُ رَبِّي ﴿٣٨﴾

42 وَتَظُنُّونَ بِٱللَّهِ ٱلظُّنُونَا۠ ﴿١٠﴾

43 يَقُولُونَ يَٰلَيْتَنَآ أَطَعْنَا ٱللَّهَ وَأَطَعْنَا ٱلرَّسُولَا۠ ﴿٦٦﴾

44 وَقَالُواْ رَبَّنَآ إِنَّآ أَطَعْنَا سَادَتَنَا وَكُبَرَآءَنَا فَأَضَلُّونَا ٱلسَّبِيلَا۠ ﴿٦٧﴾

45 وَيُطَافُ عَلَيْهِم بِـَٔانِيَةٍ مِّن فِضَّةٍ وَأَكْوَابٍ كَانَتْ قَوَارِيرَا۠ verse 15. As for the second incidence of *qawārīra*, which appears in verse 16, the *alif* is omitted whether stopping or continuing.

46 إِنَّآ أَعْتَدْنَا لِلْكَٰفِرِينَ سَلَٰسِلَا۠ وَأَغْلَٰلًا وَسَعِيرًا ﴿٤﴾

Subtle Pauses (*al-Sakta al-Laṭīfa*)

Definition

The subtle pause is the interruption of the voice upon pronunciation of a *sākin* letter where the period of time paused is less than it would be for a regular stop. No breath is inhaled or exhaled and the intention is to immediately resume the recitation.

Locations It Appears

It is required in four places in the Holy Quran according to Ḥafṣ from the Shāṭibiyya method:

1. وَلَمْ يَجْعَل لَّهُۥ عِوَجَاۜ[47] ۝١ قَيِّمًا لِّيُنذِرَ بَأْسًا شَدِيدًا *(al-Kahf 1-2)*
2. قَالُوا۟ يَٰوَيْلَنَا مَنۢ بَعَثَنَا مِن مَّرْقَدِنَاۜ هَٰذَا مَا وَعَدَ ٱلرَّحْمَٰنُ *(Yāsīn 52)*
3. وَقِيلَ مَنْۜ رَاقٍ *(al-Qiyāma 27)*
4. كَلَّا بَلْۜ رَانَ عَلَىٰ قُلُوبِهِم مَّا كَانُوا۟ يَكْسِبُونَ *(al-Muṭaffifīn 14)*

[47] It is permissible for the Ḥafṣ reader to pause at عوجا because it is the last word of the verse in this case without the subtle pause, but if the reader continues, then they must pause.

If the pause is not observed, it is possible, according to Ḥafṣ from Ṭayyiba, to follow the rule of *idghām* instead (من رَّاق، بل رَّان) for whomever recites using shortened (*qaṣr*) elongations.

There are two places where this pause is possible:

1. مَآ أَغْنَىٰ عَنِّي مَالِيَهْ ۜ ﴿٢٨﴾ هَلَكَ عَنِّي سُلْطَٰنِيَهْ ﴿٢٩﴾ (*al-Ḥāqqa 28–29*)
   It is permissible to blend (*idghām*) the (ها) of (ماليه) with (هلك) to become (ماليهَّلك), but even so, a pause is preferable.

2. (...عَلِيمٌ بَرَآءَةٌ...) In the case of continued recitation from Sūrat al-Anfāl to the beginning of Sūrat al-Tawba, pause at the *mīm* in (عليمْ) a subtle pause, then begin with (براءة).

Reason for the Pause

It could be for the meaning, as in the first and second example. Or it could be for negation as in the third example (لا أحد يرقى), or it could be didactic, as in the fourth example.

The Two *Hamzas*: *Waṣl* and *Qaṭʿa*

A *hamza* in the beginning of a word will be either *hamzat waṣl* or *qaṭʿa*.

Hamzat Qaṭʿa

That which is vocalized both when attached to and when beginning a word.

a. Its Name

It is called *hamzat qaṭʿa* because it separates the letter before it from the letter after it.

b. Its Occurrence

It occurs where *hamzat waṣl* does not.

Hamzat Waṣl

That which is vocalized when begun with and not vocalized in the midst of recitation. It is known that one cannot begin except with a letter that is *mutaḥarrik*. So the first word, if it is *sākin,* needs a *hamzat waṣl* to make its enunciation possible.

a. Its Name

It is called *hamzat waṣl* because with it, one can pronounce a letter with a *sukūn* and because it is easy for the tongue. Thus, it is called a step ladder for the tongue.

b. Location

It is found in nouns, verbs, and prepositions. It is not found, however, in the present tense, nor in the past tense of verbs with three or four root letters. (أكل، أجاب)

So it is found:

1. In the definite article (الـ)
2. In the past tense of verbs with five root letters (انتقل), verbs with six root letters (استغفر), their imperatives (اِنتقل، اِستغفر), their gerunds (اِنتقال، اِستغفار), and the imperative form of verbs with three root letters (اِذْهَبْ، اِضْرِبْ، اُدْخُلْ)
3. The following seven nouns as they appear in the Quran: اِبن، اِبنة، اِمرؤ، اِمرأة، اِثنان، اِثنتان، اِسم

c. Its *Ḥaraka* (Diacritical Mark)[48]

If it begins a word:

1. Fatḥa: If it appears on the definite article (الـ)
2. Kasra:
   a. The past tense and imperative form of verbs built on five or six root letters. اِنتقل، اِنتقلْ اِستغفرَ، اِستغفرْ
   b. The imperative form of verbs with three root letters, if the third letter has a *kasra* or a *fatḥa*. اِذْهَبْ، اِضْرِبْ
   c. The imperative verb if the third letter has a nonoriginal *ḍamma*. For example, اِمشُوا its original form is امشيوا. The *kasra* of the *shīn* was exchanged for a *ḍamma* as it is the *ḥaraka* that relates to the *waw*. Similarly, اِهدُوا- اِيْتوا- اِقضوا.
   d. In gerunds that are five or six letters and are not linked to the definitive article (الـ). For example, اِنتقال، اِستغفار
   e. In the ten nouns that follow. Seven appear in the Quran: اِبن، اِبنة، اِمرؤ، اِمرأة، اِثنان، اِثنتان، اِسم . These three do not: اِبنُم، اِيم، اِست.
3. Ḍamma:
   a. Passive past tense verbs based on five or six letters. اُجتُثّت، اُستُخرِج
   b. Imperative verbs based on three letters, if the third letter originally carries a *ḍamma*. اُنظُر، اُعبُد

In short, the *ḥaraka* of a *hamzat waṣl* is:

1. *Fatḥa*: If it begins the definitive article ال: اَلحمد، اَلعالمين
2. *Ḍamma*: If the third letter of the word has an original *ḍamma*: اُعبُد، اُضطُرَّ، اُمتُحن
3. *Kasra*: Any other case

[48] The *ḥaraka* of the *hamzat waṣl* is changeable because it is not from the original form of the word.

Note #1: If a *hamza* that indicates a question is placed before a *hamzat waṣl* that is not a *hamzat waṣl* of the definite article, the *hamzat waṣl* is omitted and the *hamza* that indicates a question remains with a *fatḥa*. This can be found in the Quran in seven cases:

قُلْ أَتَّخَذْتُمْ عِندَ ٱللَّهِ عَهْدًا (أَتَّخَذْتُمْ its original form is أَٱتخذتم) *(al-Baqara 80)*

أَطَّلَعَ ٱلْغَيْبَ *(Maryam 78)*

أَفْتَرَىٰ عَلَى ٱللَّهِ كَذِبًا *(Saba' 8)*

أَصْطَفَى ٱلْبَنَاتِ عَلَى ٱلْبَنِينَ *(al-Ṣāffāt 153)*

أَتَّخَذْنَـٰهُمْ سِخْرِيًّا *(Ṣād 63)*

أَسْتَكْبَرْتَ أَمْ كُنتَ مِنَ ٱلْعَالِينَ *(Ṣād 75)*

سَوَآءٌ عَلَيْهِمْ أَسْتَغْفَرْتَ لَهُمْ *(al-Munāfiqūn 6)*

Note #2: If a word ends with a *sukūn* and the word following it has a *hamzat waṣl*, the letter carrying the *sukūn* takes on a *ḥaraka* in order to avoid the pronunciation problem of two consecutive *sākin* letters.

1. <u>With a *kasra*</u>: Used on the basis of avoiding two *sākin* letters together and it is the most common solution.
   (قلْ الحمدُ الله ← قُلِ ٱلْحَمْدُ لِلَّهِ) *(Luqmān 25)*
   (أحدُنِ الله الصّمد) ← (قُلْ هُوَ ٱللَّهُ أَحَدٌ ۝١ ٱللَّهُ ٱلصَّمَدُ ۝٢) *(al-Ikhlāṣ 1-2)*

2. <u>With a *ḍamma*</u>: If the letter carrying a *sukūn* is a *mīm* that indicates a possessive plural pronoun.
   (حَرَّم عليكمْ الميتة) ← (إِنَّمَا حَرَّمَ عَلَيْكُمُ ٱلْمَيْتَةَ وَٱلدَّمَ) *(al-Baqara 173)*
   (لهمْ البشرى) ← (لَهُمُ ٱلْبُشْرَىٰ فِى ٱلْحَيَوٰةِ ٱلدُّنْيَا) *(Yūnus 64)*
   (و لا يُسأل عن ذنوبهمْ المجرمون) ← (وَلَا يُسْـَٔلُ عَن ذُنُوبِهِمُ ٱلْمُجْرِمُونَ) *(al-Qaṣaṣ 78)*
   If the letter that is *sākin* is the plural *waw* and all preceding letters have a *fatḥa*.
   (ولا تنسَوْا الفضل بينكم) ← (وَلَا تَنسَوُاْ ٱلْفَضْلَ بَيْنَكُمْ) *(al-Baqara 237)*

3. <u>With a *fatḥa*</u>: In the opening verse of Sūrat Āl ʿImrān, the *mīm* takes a *fatḥa* when the reader continues their recitation (without stopping) to His glorious name.
   (الٓمٓ ۝١ ٱللَّهُ لَآ إِلَـٰهَ إِلَّا هُوَ ٱلْحَىُّ ٱلْقَيُّومُ ۝٢) *(Āl ʿImrān 1-2)*
   Also when (مِنْ) the preposition precedes the definite article (الـ) it takes a *fatḥa*.
   (و ما كان مِنْ المنتصرين) ← (وَمَا كَانَ مِنَ ٱلْمُنتَصِرِينَ) *(al-Qaṣaṣ 81)*

Waqf (Stopping) and *Ibtidā*ʾ (Starting)

Waqf and *ibtidā*ʾ are some of the most important rules of the art of reciting, and the reader should take care to follow them. Sayyidina ʿAlī ﵁ was asked about the verse (وَرَتِّلِ ٱلْقُرْءَانَ تَرْتِيلًا) *(al-Muzzammil 4)* ("and recite the Quran in *tartīl*"), and he answered, "[it is] the beautiful articulation and pronunciation of the letters and the knowledge about when to pause and stop."

There are several reasons for stopping during recitation.

1. Forced/unplanned: Stopping due to running out of breath, coughing, or forgetfulness. It is permissible on any word.
2. Informative: Stopping purposefully wherein the reciter is examined (as in a test).
3. Voluntary: Stopping at will.

It is this voluntary type of stopping that is regulated by rules.

Definition of *Waqf*

Linguistically: Cessation/stoppage.

Technically: Cutting off of the voice at the end of a word that allows the reader to breathe, usually with the intention of continuing the reading.

Place of *Waqf*

At the end of a word or the end of that which is connected to it in script.

The Four Categories of *Waqf*

1. *Waqf Tām* (Complete)
2. *Waqf Kāfī* (Sufficient)
3. *Waqf Ḥasan* (Acceptable)
4. *Waqf Qabīḥ* (Unacceptable)

1. *Waqf Tām* (Complete Stop)

That is stopping at a point where the meaning is clear and complete, and the word that follows is not connected in pronunciation (grammatically) or meaning.

Rule: It is acceptable to stop here and acceptable to begin with what follows.

Example: Stopping at (وَإِيَّاكَ نَسْتَعِينُ) *(al-Fātiḥa 5)* and at (وَأُوْلَٰٓئِكَ هُمُ ٱلْمُفْلِحُونَ) *(al-Baqara 5)*.

Indications

1. It is the end of a story.
2. When what begins after it is a command in the negative form.
   وَٱللَّهُ عِندَهُۥ حُسْنُ ٱلثَّوَابِ ﴿١٩٥﴾ لَا يَغُرَّنَّكَ تَقَلُّبُ ٱلَّذِينَ كَفَرُواْ فِي ٱلْبِلَٰدِ ﴿١٩٦﴾
   (Āl ʿImrān 195–196)
3. When what begins after the stop is a conditional phrase.
   لَّيْسَ بِأَمَانِيِّكُمْ وَلَآ أَمَانِيِّ أَهْلِ ٱلْكِتَٰبِۗ مَن يَعْمَلْ سُوٓءًا يُجْزَ بِهِۦ *(al-Nisāʾ 123)*
4. When a question begins immediately following a stop.
   ٱللَّهُ يَحْكُمُ بَيْنَكُمْ يَوْمَ ٱلْقِيَٰمَةِ فِيمَا كُنتُمْ فِيهِ تَخْتَلِفُونَ ﴿٦٩﴾ أَلَمْ تَعْلَمْ أَنَّ ٱللَّهَ يَعْلَمُ
   (al-Ḥajj 69–70)
5. When an imperative begins after the stop.
   لَا يَمَسُّهُمْ فِيهَا نَصَبٌ وَمَا هُم مِّنْهَا بِمُخْرَجِينَ ﴿٤٨﴾ * نَبِّئْ عِبَادِيٓ أَنِّيٓ أَنَا ٱلْغَفُورُ ٱلرَّحِيمُ
   (al-Ḥijr 48–49)
6. Beginning immediately with a *yā* (يا) of addressing someone.
   إِنَّ ٱللَّهَ عَلَىٰ كُلِّ شَيْءٖ قَدِيرٞ ﴿٢٠﴾ يَٰٓأَيُّهَا ٱلنَّاسُ ٱعْبُدُواْ رَبَّكُمُ *(al-Baqara 20–21)*
7. Separation between verses about punishment and verses about mercy
   فَإِن لَّمْ تَفْعَلُواْ وَلَن تَفْعَلُواْ فَٱتَّقُواْ ٱلنَّارَ ٱلَّتِي وَقُودُهَا ٱلنَّاسُ وَٱلْحِجَارَةُۖ أُعِدَّتْ لِلْكَٰفِرِينَ ﴿٢٤﴾
   وَبَشِّرِ ٱلَّذِينَ ءَامَنُواْ وَعَمِلُواْ ٱلصَّٰلِحَٰتِ *(al-Baqara 24–25)*
8. Transfer from descriptive statements to the actual account.
   وَمِن قَوْمِ مُوسَىٰٓ أُمَّةٞ يَهْدُونَ بِٱلْحَقِّ وَبِهِۦ يَعْدِلُونَ ﴿١٥٩﴾ وَقَطَّعْنَٰهُمُ ٱثْنَتَيْ عَشْرَةَ أَسْبَاطًا أُمَمٗاۚ
   (al-ʿArāf 159–160)

2. *Waqf Kāfī* (Sufficient Stop)

Stopping though the meaning will be continued, and so it relates to what follows it as to meaning but not as to pronunciation. Thus, stopping on the word (يؤمنون) in the following verse:

(إِنَّ ٱلَّذِينَ كَفَرُواْ سَوَآءٌ عَلَيْهِمْ ءَأَنذَرْتَهُمْ أَمْ لَمْ تُنذِرْهُمْ لَا يُؤْمِنُونَ) *(al-Baqara 6–7)*

because that which follows it (خَتَمَ ٱللَّهُ عَلَىٰ قُلُوبِهِمْ) is about the state of the *kāfirūn* (nonbelievers) and thus a continuation of the intended meaning.

Placement: Repeated places in the breaks of the verses.

Rule: Acceptable to stop at it and begin with what follows it.

3. *Waqf Ḥasan* (Acceptable Stop)

Definition: A stop where the meaning is incomplete and it is connected to what follows it in meaning and pronunciation.

Rule: It is acceptable to stop, but not acceptable to begin with what follows it. The word that was stopped upon must be reread or a word before that, so that the meaning is guaranteed. This applies unless the stop is at the last word of a verse because the Prophet ﷺ used to stop at the last words of verses without returning to repeat a word.

Example:

ٱلْحَمْدُ لِلَّهِ رَبِّ ٱلْعَٰلَمِينَ *(al-Fātiḥa 2)*

Readers may stop at (ٱلْحَمْدُ لِلَّهِ), but they must repeat it to continue.

ٱلْحَمْدُ لِلَّهِ رَبِّ ٱلْعَٰلَمِينَ ﴿٢﴾ ٱلرَّحْمَٰنِ ٱلرَّحِيمِ ﴿٣﴾ *(al-Fātiḥa 2–3)*

Whereas stopping at (الْعَالَمِينَ) and beginning with (ٱلرَّحْمَٰنِ ٱلرَّحِيمِ) is acceptable without repeating it because it is the end of a verse.

It could be that to stop is acceptable, but to begin after it is unacceptable. For example, يُخْرِجُونَ ٱلرَّسُولَ وَإِيَّاكُمْ ۙ أَن تُؤْمِنُواْ بِٱللَّهِ رَبِّكُمْ *(al-Mumtaḥina 1)*. It is not permitted to begin with (وَإِيَّاكُم).

4. *Waqf Qabīḥ* (Unacceptable Stop)

Stopping in a place where the meaning is incomplete.

Rule: It is not permissible to stop. One may stop out of necessity—as in running out of breath or sneezing or yawning, in which case it is obligatory to return to that which is before it that will connect to what follows so that the meaning is correct and clear.

Indications: For the reader to stop at the subject (of a sentence) without its predicate or at a verb without its object or at a preposition without the word it modifies. The worst stop is for the reader to stop in a place so that a meaning that was not intended by Allah ﷻ is understood. For example:

(al-Nisā' 43) يَٰٓأَيُّهَا ٱلَّذِينَ ءَامَنُواْ لَا تَقْرَبُواْ ٱلصَّلَوٰةَ[9] ° وَأَنتُمْ سُكَٰرَىٰ

(Yūsuf 17) وَتَرَكْنَا يُوسُفَ عِندَ مَتَٰعِنَا فَأَكَلَهُ ° ٱلذِّئْبُ

The absolute worst, most unacceptable stop is to stop at a word that infers an understanding that is outside of the Islamic tenets of faith (*ʿaqīda*) and infers an attribute that is not worthy of Allah ﷻ:

(Muḥammad 19) فَٱعْلَمْ أَنَّهُۥ لَآ إِلَٰهَ ° إِلَّا ٱللَّهُ

(al-Aḥqāf 10) إِنَّ ٱللَّهَ لَا يَهْدِى ° ٱلْقَوْمَ ٱلظَّٰلِمِينَ

(al-Baqara 26) إِنَّ ٱللَّهَ لَا يَسْتَحْيِۦٓ ° أَن يَضْرِبَ مَثَلًا مَّا بَعُوضَةً

Note: The scholars have agreed that stopping before the beginning of a new verse is sunna, but they have differed as to the breaks of meaning. Of these differences is the permissibility of stopping between:

(al-Māʿūn 5–4) فَوَيْلٌ لِّلْمُصَلِّينَ ﴿٤﴾ ٱلَّذِينَ هُمْ عَن صَلَاتِهِمْ سَاهُونَ

An obligatory stop does not exist in the Quran. (Obligatory in the meaning that the reader who leaves it has sinned.) A reader does not sin by any stop unless the reader intentionally attempts to distort through it. The one who purposely stops on the worst of the unacceptable stops has disbelieved.

[49] ° indicates a *waqf qabīḥ*.

One will not know a correct stop unless they read with care. Allah ﷻ says:

كِتَٰبٌ أَنزَلْنَٰهُ إِلَيْكَ مُبَٰرَكٌ لِّيَدَّبَّرُوٓا۟ ءَايَٰتِهِۦ

This is a blessed Book which We have revealed to you, that they might reflect upon its verses and that those of understanding would be reminded.

(Ṣād 29)

أَفَلَا يَتَدَبَّرُونَ ٱلْقُرْءَانَ أَمْ عَلَىٰ قُلُوبٍ أَقْفَالُهَآ

Will they not, then, ponder over this Quran—or are there locks upon their hearts?

(Muḥammad 24)

ʿAlī ﵁ said: "There is no goodness in worship that is devoid of *fiqh* (a legal system) nor in recitation that is devoid of reflection."

Qaṭʿa: A Radical Stop

A purposeful stop of the recitation with an intention of ending the reading, and that cannot occur except for at the end of a verse. If the reader returns again to the recitation, they must seek refuge in Allah ﷻ again: أَعُوذُ بِاللّهِ مِنَ الشَّيطَانِ الرَّجِيم

Beginning

Personal choice: It is permissible to begin from any verse as long as the words denote the intended and beneficial meaning (as opposed to beginning at a verse that—because the previous verse is left out—distorts the intended meaning). It is not permissible to begin from a verse if it distorts the meaning. Some verses that should not be begun with in order not to distort the meaning follow:[50]

إِنَّ ٱللَّهَ ثَالِثُ ثَلَٰثَةٍ *(al-Māʾida 73)*

وَإِيَّاكُمْ أَن تُؤْمِنُوا۟ بِٱللَّهِ رَبِّكُمْ *(al-Mumtaḥina 1)*

إِنَّ ٱللَّهَ فَقِيرٌ وَنَحْنُ أَغْنِيَآءُ *(Āl ʿImrān 181)*

---

[50] Note: The types of stops differ according to the difference in explanation or recitations. For example, Allah ﷻ says:

(وَمَا يَعْلَمُ تَأْوِيلَهُۥٓ إِلَّا ٱللَّهُ stop وَٱلرَّٰسِخُونَ فِى ٱلْعِلْمِ يَقُولُونَ ءَامَنَّا بِهِۦ) *(Āl ʿImrān 7)*

This is a *waqf tām* (complete) for those who explain that the *waw* is a *waw istiʿnāfiyya* (or one that causes a break in meaning). The *waqf* is *ḥasan* for those who consider it to be a *waw ʿaṭf* (or a conjunction *waw* that joins phrases together to create one meaning).

Ishmām and *Rawm*

Ishmām and *rawm* are two types of stops (*waqf*). Their purpose is to show the original *ḥaraka* that is on the word that has been stopped on (and therefore given a *sukūn*).[51]

Ishmām

A sign of the *ḍamma*, which is formed by the lips without vocalization, is made to signify the original *ḥaraka* of the word. It only occurs in the case of a *ḍamma* (ُ). The word *ishmām* is derived from the word "*sham*" or "scent." That is, the letter is provided with a reminder of its *ḥaraka* by preparing the organs of speech to pronounce it.

a. The Purpose

To differentiate between that which is *mutaḥarrik* in a continued reading and *sākin* upon stopping and that which is *sākin* in all cases.

نستعينُ، يقبضُ، حيثُ، الصَّمدُ، بقيَّتُ

The *ishmām* is pronounced in the case of *al-qaṣr* (two counts) or *tawassuṭ* (four) or *ṭawīl* (six). So the rule of elongation with *ishmām* is the same as the rule for a regular stop.

b. The Method

Place the lips in the position of a *ḍamma* upon pronunciation of the final letter, which originally carried a *ḍamma* but is *sākin* because of the stop. Do not vocalize the *ḍamma*, but place the lips in the position after pronouncing

[51] *Ishmām* and *rawm* are not applicable to plural *mīm* or plural *waw* (لا تنسَوُا الفضلَ بينكم) (أنتم الأعْلَون) because the *ḍamma* is extraneous to the word. They are not applicable to ة *tā' marbūṭa* either because the *tā'* in this case becomes a *hā'* when stopped on.

the last letter (without extending it). If one stops and extends it, then it is a pure stop without *ishmām*. So for example, when stopping at (نستعينُ), a *sukūn* is placed on the *nūn* and the *yā'* is lengthened to the length of *'āriḍ li-l-sukūn* as it relates to *madd ṭabī'ī* or mid-length or lengthened elongation. The lips form the *ḍamma* after the *nūn* but do not pronounce it. If the last letter of the word is a letter of *qalqala*, then upon stopping with *ishmām*, the clear *qalqala* is considered (نعبدُ).

Upon pronunciation of the word (تأمنّا)[52] with *ishmām*, the lips are formed as a *ḍamma* (without vocalization) after the *sukūn* on the first *nūn* and the *idghām* of the second (which is complete) and before the completion of the *shadda* (or before the complete pronunciation of *nūn* with a *shadda*). The *ishmām* here is like the *ishmām* of stopping on a *ḍamma* because the first *nūn* was originally so (تأمَنُنا), but became *sākina* in *idghām*.

Rawm

It is the vocalization of a portion of the *ḥaraka*. Some say one-third, leaving aside the remaining two-thirds. That is in the case where a word is stopped upon and the reader concurrently attempts to make known the original *ḥaraka*. This applies whether the final letter has a *ḍamma* or a *kasra*, has a *shadda* or does not, with *tanwīn* or without it. If it has *tanwīn*, one must ignore it if stopping in a manner of *rawm*. For example: (نستعينُ، حميدٍ، رحمتُ، قبلُ، و العصرِ). With *rawm*, the *madd* is lengthened to two counts (as it is in a continued reading) and followed with a part of a *ḍamma*.

[52] *Ishmām* and *rawm* are necessary for the word (تأمنّا) in all of the various readings, except for Abū Ja'far—he does pure *idghām* without any exchange (مالك لا تأمنّا). As for Ḥafṣ, *ishmām* is not found in the middle of any other word besides (تأمنّا).

	Ishmām	*Rawm*
1	The letter is pronounced with *sukūn*, then the lips are placed in the position of a *ḍamma* without extending it.	The letter is pronounced with a part of its *ḥaraka*.
2	It is without sound, and therefore can only be seen by those with sight and not by the blind.	It has a soft sound that can only be heard by the near and not the distant.
3	It only occurs where there is a *ḍamma* at the end of the word.	It occurs where there is either a *ḍamma* or a *kasra* at the end of the word.
4	It operates the same as, and includes all of the rules of, a regular stop. (A *madd* preceding it is *madd ʿāriḍ li-l-sukūn* and the *qalqala* remains if one of its letters is stopped on with *ishmām*.)	It operates the same as, and includes all of the rules of, a continuation. (A *madd* preceding it remains *madd ṭabīʿī*.)

Symbols for Stops and Other Technical Indicators

Technical indicators of stops did not exist in the Muṣḥaf al-Imām,[53] but they were added by scholars to make it easier for the reader to know places where it is permissible and prohibited to stop. They are not found in every *muṣḥaf*. In fact, they differ, and can be fewer or greater from *muṣḥaf* to *muṣḥaf*. That is why some of the *muṣḥafs* have lists wherein they mention the signs at the back. It is preferred that one takes into account the meaning when considering where and when to stop. The most important indicators are:

م	Necessary stop
لا	Prohibited stop
ج	Permissible stop; may either stop or continue
صلى	Permissible stop; continuing is better
قلى	Permissible stop; stopping is better

[53] Muṣḥaf al-Imām: It is the original directed writing that was written and copied by Sayyidina ʿUthmān ibn ʿAffān رضي الله عنه and distributed to the major regions (Bosra, Syria or Damascus, Mecca, Medina [public], Medina [governmental], Yemen, and Bahrain).

ۛ	Inclusive stop: each sign is put on one of two nearby words; if the first is stopped upon, then the second is not. It is not permissible to stop on both ذَٰلِكَ ٱلْكِتَـٰبُ لَا رَيْبَ ۛ فِيهِ ۛ هُدًى لِّلْمُتَّقِينَ *(al-Baqara 2)*
۟	A zero indicates an extra letter and it is not pronounced سَأُو۟رِيكُمْ *(al-'Arāf 37)*
ۦ ۥ ۨ	Miniature letters; placed to point out the pronunciation of a letter that is not written مَا وُۥرِىَ *(al-'Arāf 20)* يَلْوُۥنَ أَلْسِنَتَهُم *(Āl 'Imrān 78)* إِۦلَـٰفِهِمْ رِحْلَةَ ٱلشِّتَآءِ *(Quraysh 2)* إِنَّ وَلِـِّۧىَ ٱللَّهُ *(al-'Arāf 196)* وَكَذَٰلِكَ نُـۨجِى ٱلْمُؤْمِنِينَ *(al-Anbiyā' 88)*
●	A circle placed under the word indicates that its sound is between *yā'* and *alif* مَجْر۪ىٰهَا *(Hūd 41)* A circle placed over the word points out *ishmām* and *rawm* تَأْمَ۫نَّا *(Yūsuf 11)*
ۜ	A small *sīn* indicates a pause

The Design of the *Muṣḥaf*

It is unanimously agreed that it is haram to write out a *muṣḥaf* in a way other than that which was originally written in the time period of ʿUthmān ibn ʿAffān (may Allah be pleased with him). Some opinions were put forth that the ornamentation of the Quran for the purpose of learning was acceptable (though it is a weak opinion). In any case, the reader must take into account the Uthmanic script, which is clarified in the following ways:

1. Separated and connected: In the Uthmanic style, the words are written in two ways—separated from and connected to each other. So if a word is written so that it is separated from others, this indicates that the reader may stop at it (in the case of teaching, loss of breath, or scrutiny). For example, one may stop at the word أن when it is written أَنْ لا.

   If, however, it is written so that the words are connected, then the reader may not stop until the connection ends. For example: ألّا، إنَّما.

2. Elision and affirmation: If the last letter of a word that is stopped upon has a *madd* letter that is affirmed by the Uthmanic script, then it is stopped upon and the letter is clearly pronounced. If the reader must stop in the example (يَـٰٓأَيُّهَا ٱلَّذِينَ ءَامَنُوا...), it would be (يا أيّها). If part of a word is omitted in the script of the *muṣḥaf*, then the stop would be according to that omission. For example, in (يَـٰٓأَيُّهَ ٱلسَّاحِرُ) or (أَيُّهَ ٱلْمُؤْمِنُونَ), the reader stops on (أَيُّهَ) according to the way it is scripted. In the following verses (إِن تَرَنِ أَنَا۠ أَقَلَّ) (رَبِّىٓ أَكْرَمَنِ مِنكَ), the reader stops on the *nūn* with a *sukūn* according to the script.
3. The *tāʾ* that indicates feminine gender: This type of *tāʾ* is pronounced (upon stopping) according to its script. If it is written ت, then it is pronounced as a *tāʾ* with a *sukūn* (رحمتْ), as in the verse (أَهُمْ يَقْسِمُونَ رَحْمَتَ رَبِّكَ) *(al-Zukhruf 32)*. If it is written ة, then it is read as a ه when stopped at. For example, (نعمهْ), as in the verse (إِذَا خَوَّلَهُۥ نِعْمَةً[54] مِّنْهُ) *(al-Zumar 8)*.

[54] The *tanwīn* is omitted whether it is a *tanwīn* of the *fatḥa* or *ḍamma* or *kasra*.

Gross and Subtle Error

Gross Error

A mistake in the pronunciation whereby the meaning is clearly changed. For example, exchanging one letter for another, one vowel for another, or ignoring the elongation (*madd ṭabīʿī*).

Subtle Error

A mistake that causes incomplete perfection. For example, a lack of uniformity in the length of a particular *madd* by decreasing half a degree, increasing half a degree, or simply being unequal in the length of a particular *madd* in the same reading. Subtle error also includes laxity in implementing the manners of articulation (*ṣifāt*) and practicing the rules. Laxity, for example, in trilling the *rāʾ*, thickening the *lām* where it shouldn't be thickened, pronouncing the *ḍamma* in a manner that it is somewhere between a *ḍamma* and a *fatḥa* by not pursing and thrusting one's lips forward as is especially needed in the following words: (قُلْ، أَنتُم، عليكُم). Likewise, pronouncing the *kasra* so that it sounds in between a *kasra* and a *fatḥa*, is also considered a subtle error, especially in the words (عليهِم، بِهْ).

Notes Pertaining to the Recitation of *Ḥafṣ*

1. Ḥafṣ reads the following words with a *sīn*:
   وَٱللَّهُ يَقْبِضُ وَيَبْصُۜطُ *(al-Baqara 245)*
   وَزَادَهُۥ بَسْطَةً فِي ٱلْعِلْمِ وَٱلْجِسْمِۖ *(al-Baqara 247)*
   وَزَادَكُمْ فِي ٱلْخَلْقِ بَصْۜطَةًۖ *(al-ʿArāf 69)*
2. And reads with a *ṣād*:
   لَّسْتَ عَلَيْهِم بِمُصَيْطِرٍ *(al-Ghāshiya 22)*
3. Reads with a *ṣād* or a *sīn* in (المصيطرون). The pronunciation with the *ṣād* is more common.
4. The word (ضعف)[55] as it appears in three places in the Quran is read by Ḥafṣ either with a *fatḥa* on the *ḍād* or with a *ḍamma* on the *ḍād*. The *fatḥa* is more common.
5. The word (مَجْرٜىٰهَا) *(Hud 41)* is read by Ḥafṣ with a diphthong of the *alif* after the *rā'*, and with that, the *rā'* is *muraqqaqa* (in this case, the diphthong is the vowel sound between *alif* and *yā'*).
6. The word (ءَاعْجَمِيٌّ) *(Fuṣṣilat 44)* in the original form has two *hamzas* with a *ḥaraka*. The first is for the question and the second is part of the word. Ḥafṣ eases into the second *hamza* and leaves only one.

55 ٱللَّهُ ٱلَّذِى خَلَقَكُم مِّن ضَعْفٍ ثُمَّ جَعَلَ مِنۢ بَعْدِ ضَعْفٍ قُوَّةً ثُمَّ جَعَلَ مِنۢ بَعْدِ قُوَّةٍ ضَعْفًا وَشَيْبَةًۚ يَخْلُقُ مَا يَشَآءُۖ وَهُوَ ٱلْعَلِيمُ ٱلْقَدِيرُ *(Rūm 54)*

7. The pronunciation of (ءَاتَىٰنِۦَ) *(Naml 36)* has two possibilities when stopping. The first is affirmation of the *yā'* with a *sukūn*. The second is omission of the *yā'* by stopping at *nūn*. If reading is continued, the *yā'* is confirmed with a *fatḥa*.

8. Ḥafṣ reads the *mīm* with a *kasra* in the following verses:
   وَمِنْ خِزْيِ يَوْمِئِذٍ *(Hūd 66)*
   يُبَصَّرُونَهُمْ يَوَدُّ ٱلْمُجْرِمُ لَوْ يَفْتَدِى مِنْ عَذَابِ يَوْمِئِذٍ بِبَنِيهِ *(al-Ma'ārij 11)*

9. Ḥafṣ reads with a *fatḥa* on the *yā'* and a *kasra* on the ha:
   أَفَمَن يَهْدِىٓ إِلَى ٱلْحَقِّ أَحَقُّ أَن يُتَّبَعَ أَمَّن لَّا يَهِدِّىٓ إِلَّآ[6] أَن يُهْدَىٰ *(Yūnus 35)*

10. Ḥafṣ puts a *ḍamma* on the *hā'* in the word:
   وَمَنْ أَوْفَىٰ بِمَا عَـٰهَدَ[7] عَلَيْهُ ٱللَّهَ *(al-Fatḥ 10)*
   وَمَآ أَنسَـٰنِيهُ *(al-Kahf 63)*

[56] The word was (يهدّي أي يهتدي). The *tā'* is combined with the *dāl* and the two *sākin* letters have been combined so a *kasra* is added to the *hā'* in order to separate the two *sākins*.

[57] It is read with a *ḍamma* because in the original form there is a *ḍamma*. Usually in the masculine form, the *hā'* is read كتابه and in the feminine form كتابها. In other cases, it is pronounced with a *kasra* according to the preceding *yā'*.

General Notes

There are three possible ways to open Sūrat Āl ʿImrān correctly:

1. If the reader stops at the *mīm*, it is recited as (الم) in Sūrat al-Baqara or al-Sajda, such that the *alif* is elongated in the word (لام) to a *madd lāzim* and the *yā'* in the word *mīm* (ميم) to a *madd lāzim* with the *idghām* of the *mīm* between *lām* and *mīm* (the spelling of the letter words).
2. If the reader wishes to continue, then two *sākin* letters are brought together—the *sukūn* of the word *mīm* and the *sukūn* of the lam in the utterance of His glorified name (الله). Therefore, a *fatḥa* is added to the *mīm* in order to avoid the double *sukūn*. So the *ḥaraka* of the *hamza* has moved to the *mīm* and then the *mīm* follows the rule of a *madd ṭabīʿī* because the reason for the *madd lāzim* has been eliminated (the *sukūn* was exchanged for a *fatḥa*). Such is the method that relies on temporary diacritical marks.
3. There is also the opinion that in spite of the *fatḥa* on the *mīm*, the *yā'* is lengthened to a *madd lāzim*—six counts. The reason is that the *fatḥa* on the *mīm* is a substitute, and this is the opinion that one must not rely on a temporary *ḥaraka*.

There are three possible ways to connect Sūrat al-Anfāl with Sūrat al-Tawba without the *basmala*:

1. Stop at the end of al-Anfāl (عليمْ), then begin with (براءة) without the *basmala*.
2. Connect between (عَلِيمٌ) and (براءة) by pronouncing the *iqlāb*.
3. A subtle pause between (عليمٌ) and (براءة).

It is necessary that the reader takes care to make clear the following:

- A *ḍād* with a *sukūn* that appears before a *ṭā'*. For example, فمنِ اضْطُرَّ

- A *ẓā'* with a *sukūn* that appears before a *ṭā'*. For example, قَالُوا۟ سَوَآءٌ عَلَيْنَآ أَوَعَظْتَ أَمْ لَمْ تَكُن مِّنَ ٱلْوَٰعِظِينَ *(al-Shu'arā' 136)*

Recitation practice can be done in the following ways:

- An abundance of listening to correct pronunciation
- An abundance of practicing pronunciation and the rules with exercises

How to connect and stop when there is a sura that begins with letters:

- It is best to connect when the sura begins with one or two letters and they are followed by an oath. For example, ق - ن - يس والقرآن
- When connecting, *idghām* and *ikhfā'* must be pronounced. This is the case except for the *nūn* in (يس) (the word *sīn*) and the *nūn* in Sūrat al-Qalam (والقلم). Here the *idghām* is not followed.
- When a sura opens with two letters or more, and they are not followed by an oath, then either continuing or stopping is acceptable.

  As in the beginning of Sūrat al-Naml:

  طسٓ تِلْكَ ءَايَٰتُ ٱلْقُرْءَانِ وَكِتَابٍ مُّبِينٍ

  Here the *ṭā'* has a *madd ṭabī'ī* and the *sīn* has an *ikhfā'* of the *nūn* with the *tā'*. Readers may either stop on the *sīn* or continue, in which case the *nūn* or the *sīn* takes on *ikhfā'* and disappears into the تلك.

Specific Tips about the Pronunciation of Some Words

Word	Method	Location
دِينًا قِيَمًا	With a *kasra* on the *qāf* (ق) and a *fatḥa* on the *yā'* (ى)	al-An'ām 161
سَأَصْرِفُ عَنْ ءَايَٰتِيَ ٱلَّذِينَ	With a *fatḥa* on the *yā'* (ى)	al-'Arāf 146
وَقَطَّعْنَٰهُمُ ٱثْنَتَىْ عَشْرَةَ أَسْبَاطًا	(هُمُ ٱثْنَتَىْ عَشْرَةَ) Notice the *sukūn* on the *shīn* (ش)	al-'Arāf 160
إِنَّ وَلِـِّۧىَ ٱللَّهُ	Read it as (وليّي) with two *yā's*	al-'Arāf 196
مَا لَكُم مِّن وَلَٰيَتِهِم	With a *fatḥa* on the *waw* (و)	al-Anfāl 72

إِنَّمَا ٱلنَّسِيٓءُ زِيَادَةٌ فِي ٱلْكُفْرِ	(يُضَلُّ) with a *ḍamma* on the *yā'* (ي) and *fatḥa* on (ض)	al-Tawba 37
أَمَّن لَّا يَهِدِّيٓ إِلَّآ أَن يُهْدَىٰ	(يَهِدِّي) A *kasra* on the *hā'* (ه) and a *shadda* on the *dāl* (د)	Yūnus 35
قَالُواْ يَٰشُعَيْبُ أَصَلَوٰتُكَ تَأْمُرُكَ	Read it (أَصلاتك)	Hūd 87
فَلَمَّا جَهَّزَهُم بِجَهَازِهِمْ	With a *fatḥa* on the *jīm* (ج)	Yūsuf 70
رُّبَمَا يَوَدُّ ٱلَّذِينَ كَفَرُواْ	(رُبَمَا) without a *shadda*	al-Ḥijr 2
يَتَفَيَّؤُاْ ظِلَٰلُهُۥ	Read it as (يَتَفَيَّأُ) without a *madd*	al-Naḥl 48
وَأَجْلِبْ عَلَيْهِم بِخَيْلِكَ وَرَجِلِكَ	(رَجِلِك) A *fatḥa* on the *rā'* (ر) and *kasra* on the *jīm* (ج)	al-Isrā' 64
وَفَجَّرْنَا خِلَٰلَهُمَا نَهَرًا	*Fatḥa* on the *hā'* (ه)	al-Kahf 33
ٱشْدُدْ بِهِۦٓ أَزْرِي	*Ḍamma* on the *hamza* (ء)	Ṭāhā 31
مَآ أَخْلَفْنَا مَوْعِدَكَ بِمَلْكِنَا	(بِمَلكنا) *Fatḥa* on *mīm* (م)	Ṭāhā 87
وَشَجَرَةً تَخْرُجُ مِن طُورِ سَيْنَآءَ	(طُور) *Ḍamma* on *ṭā'* (ط) and (وسَيْناء) *Fatḥa* on *sīn* (س)	al-Mu'minūn 20
مِن كُلٍّ زَوْجَيْنِ ٱثْنَيْنِ	Notice the *tanwīn*	al-Mu'minūn 27
وَلَا تَكُن فِي ضَيْقٍ	*Fatḥa* on *ḍād* (ض)	al-Naml 70
إِنَّ فِي ذَٰلِكَ لَأٓيَٰتٍ لِّلْعَٰلِمِينَ	(لِلْعَٰلِمِينَ) *Kasra* on *lām* (ل)	al-Rūm 22
قُلْ أَرُونِيَ ٱلَّذِينَ	(أَرُونِيَ) *Fatḥa* on the (ي)	Saba' 27
وَهُمْ يَخِصِّمُونَ	*Kasra* on *khā'* (خ)	Yāsīn 49
إِنَّا بُرَءَٰٓؤُاْ مِنكُمْ	Read it (بُرَآءُ)	al-Mumtaḥina 4

That Which Helps in the Memorization of Quran

1. Never give up, be persistent, and strive against the *nafs* (the base self), putting to practice Allah's words: "And those who strive in our cause, we will certainly guide them to our path for verily Allah is with those who do what's best" *(al-'Ankabūt 69)*.
2. Divide the sura into topics, memorizing each in a single sitting (if possible), after reading it several times with understanding and trying to perceive connections between the various verses of the topic.
3. Repeat the memorized portion several times. In fact, a certain shaykh would not permit his son to memorize anything new until he had repeated what he had just memorized forty times. The son learned the Quran with perfection.
4. Avoid sin and distance the self from it and ask Allah for forgiveness if one falls into sin. One should also give in charity to purify one's heart and memory. Imam Shafi'i said: "I complained to Wakī'[58] of my poor memory. He advised me to leave all sin and told me that knowledge is light, and Allah's light is not given to a sinner."
5. Say "Allahu akbar" after each sura, beginning from the end of Sūrat al-Ḍuḥā (93) and ending after Sūrat al-Falaq (before Sūrat al-Nās).[59] The reason for this is that the revelation to the Messenger of Allah ﷺ slackened for several days, so the idol worshippers said in animosity and harassment: "Muhammad has been abandoned by his Lord and left." Therefore when Jibrīl 🕮 arrived and revealed to the Prophet ﷺ Sūrat al-Ḍuḥā in its entirety,

[58] His teacher.

[59] For the one who connects Sūrat al-Nās to Sūrat al-Fātiḥa with the intention of beginning a new *khatma*, it is acceptable to say "Allahu akbar" between them.

the Prophet said at its revelation "Allahu akbar" confirming his position with Allah ﷻ and belying the idol worshippers.

6. It is sunna for the reciter to connect Sūrat al-Nas with Sūrat al-Fātiḥa and continue to the beginning of Sūrat al-Baqara up to (وَأُوْلَٰٓئِكَ هُمُ ٱلْمُفْلِحُونَ). Ibn Abbas ؓ narrated: "A man said: 'O Messenger of Allah, what deed is most beloved to Allah?' He ﷺ said 'The one who no sooner arrives than he then departs.' He said 'Who is the one who no sooner arrives then departs?' He ﷺ answered: 'One who travels from the beginning of the Quran to the end. As soon as he arrives at the end, he starts again.'"[60] It is sunna to make *dua* (supplicate) after completing the Quran.

[60] *Sunan al-Tirmidhī,* Book of Readings, chap. 13, no. 2948.

The *Dua* of Completing the Quran[61]

O Allah, we are your servants and the children of your servants. Our foreheads are in Your hands, Your sentence is effective upon us. What you destine for us is just.

We ask You by every name that is Yours, that You have named Yourself with or revealed in Your book or taught to any of Your creatures, or held back with Yourself in the concealed knowledge, that You make the Glorious Quran the spring of our hearts, the light of our eyes, the cure of our hearts, the dispelling of our sadness, the disperser of our worries and cares, and our leader and driver to You and to Your Heavens, the Heavens of blessing and Your abode. The abode of peace with those whom You have blessed of Prophets, the righteous, martyrs, and *ṣāliḥīn* by Your Mercy, O most Merciful of the Merciful.

O Allah, grant me mercy by the Great Quran and make it my imam (leader), guidance, and blessing.

O Allah, remind me of that which I have forgotten of it. Teach me that which I do not know of it. Grant me its correct recitation in the hours of the night and the edges of the day. And make it count for me, O Lord of the worlds.

اللَّهمَّ إنَّا عبيدُك وأبناءُ عبيدِك وأبناءُ إمائك، ناصيَتُنا بيَدِك، ماضٍ فينا حكْمُك، عدلٌ فينا قضاؤك.
نَسألُكَ بكُلِّ اسمٍ هوَ لَك، سمَّيتَ بِهِ نَفسَك، أو أنزلتَهُ في كتابك، أو علَّمتَهُ أحداً من خلقك، أو اسْتَأثرتَ بهِ في علمِ الغيبِ عندَك، أن تجعلَ القرآنَ العظيمَ ربيعَ قُلوبنا، ونورَ أبصارِنا، وشِفَاءَ صُدورِنا، وجَلاءَ أحزانِنا، وذهاب همومنا وغُمومنا، وسائِقَنا وقائدَنا إليك وإلى جنَّاتِكَ، جنَّاتِ النَّعيم، ودارِكَ دارِ السَّلام معَ الذين أنعمتَ عليهم من النَّبيِّنَ والصدِّيقينَ والصَّالحين، بِرَحمتِك يا أرحمَ الرَّاحمين.

اللّهمَّ ارحمني بالقرآن، واجْعلهُ لي إماماً وهدىً ورَحمة.

اللّهمَّ ذكِّرني منه ما نَسيتُ، وعلِّمني منه ما جَهِلتُ، وارزُقني تلاوتَه
آناءَ اللَّيل وأطرافَ النَّهار، واجْعلْهُ حُجَّةَ لي يا ربَّ العالمين

[61] References are available in the original Arabic book.

The *Dua* for Not Forgetting What Has Been Memorized of the Quran

O Allah, give light with your book to my vision, and let my tongue flow with it, and expand my chest with it, and use my body with it, by your ability and strength. Verily there is no ability or strength but by You. All praise and thanks belong to Allah, the Lord of the worlds.

اللَّهمَّ نوِّر بكتابك بَصري، وأَطْلِقْ بهِ لِساني، واشرَحْ به صدْري، واستعمِلْ بهِ جَسَدي،
بحولِك وقوَّتك، فإنَّه لا حولَ ولا قوَّة إلا بك.

والحمد لله ربِّ العالمين